THE FOOD OF
VIETNAM

Authentic Recipes from the Heart of Indochina

Recipes by *Trieu Thi Choi and Marcel Isaak*
Introduction by *Annabel Jackson-Doling*
Food photography by *Heinz von Holzen*
Styling by *Christina Ong*

**PERIPLUS
EDITIONS**

Contents

Part One: Food in Vietnam

One of Asia's best kept culinary secrets—but not for long!

Vietnam is a country on the rise. An almost palpable sense of optimism hangs in the balmy air. The Vietnam War (known here as the "American War") has not been forgotten, nor have the years of oppression and foreign rule, but the country is moving on. The effects of *doi moi*, the economic reform policy allowing small-scale private enterprise, introduced by the communist government in 1986, are becoming more and more evident. The accumulation of personal wealth is now encouraged, joint ventures with overseas companies are welcomed, and many Vietnamese are returning to their country to start businesses after years abroad.

The fancy new restaurants that are restoring life to old colonial buildings, and the modern hotels steadily creeping into the skyline, are just two of the many signs signaling Vietnam's renaissance. And one needn't go farther than a few steps onto any street to experience the thriving culinary scene that is so much a part of this new vitality.

On the streets of Ho Chi Minh City or Hanoi in the early morning, food stalls appear on the sidewalks in front of old shop houses. Clusters of tiny chairs and tables surround a steaming hot cauldron of soup set on an open flame; soon the chairs will be filled with people huddled over their morning bowl of *pho*, a tasty beef broth served with rice noodles and fresh herbs. At another streetside restaurant, a team of female chefs is busy making open-faced omelets in blackened pans over small charcoal grills. Vendors with carts full of baguettes, cheese and sausages are making sandwiches and serving a refreshing beverage of young coconut. Another vendor is wrapping sticky rice in a banana leaf, and handing it to a young schoolboy who is waiting impatiently with his mother.

The markets are a hive of activity as well, literally overflowing with fresh goods trucked in from the nearby villages, the bountiful coastal waters, and the central highlands. Throughout the day, crowds of people fill their baskets from the rows of fresh vegetables and tropical fruits, live fish and game, pickled meats and vegetables, candied fruit, dried and packaged goods, rice and bottles of the pungent *nuoc mam* fish sauce.

There is a renewed vitality in Vietnam that revolves around food. At night, a seemingly endless stream of vehicles parades through the streets. Handsome young men, elegantly dressed women, young couples, and entire families speed about on motorbikes, stopping only to have a beer, talk with friends or have a meal at the literally hundreds of streetside restaurants or at fancy cafés, then race back out to join the nightly procession.

A Land of Breathtaking Contrasts

Geographical variations have created a country
of great agricultural bounty

With lengths of unspoiled dramatic coastline, sheltered harbours, fertile and well-irrigated lowlands and vast upland forests, Vietnam is a remarkably beautiful and fertile land, rich in agricultural resources. It is rapidly becoming a major supplier of rice, fish, fresh fruit and vegetables to the rest of Southeast Asia.

The Vietnamese landscape is noted for its fertility and dramatic changeability.

Vietnam's narrow curving "S" shape hugs the coast of Indochina for 1,000 miles north to south, and measures just over 30 miles across at its narrowest point. The country boasts a 1,600-mile coastline in addition to countless dikes, canals and waterways, which include the Red River, the Perfume River and the Mekong River—one of the longest rivers in Southeast Asia. It is certainly no surprise then, that seafood and aquatic life are such an integral part of the diet throughout the country.

The other essential component of the Vietnamese diet is rice. The Red River Delta in the north and the Mekong Delta in the south are the two main rice-growing areas, although lush green rice paddies dotted with water buffalo and rows of women with their distinctive conical hats can be seen throughout the country. The importance of rice to the economy is indicated by Vietnam's ranking as the third largest rice exporter in the world after Thailand and the United States, although the quality of its rice has not been regarded as highly as that of the other nations.

Sixty percent of arable land in Vietnam is given over to rice production, leaving little pasture for cattle farming. Hence beef, in particular, is a luxury for most Vietnamese, and the famous series of dishes, *bo bay mon* (literally, beef done seven ways), is highly regarded. In spite of urbanization and increasingly populated cities, roughly 80 percent of the population relies on rice for its livelihood.

The applications of rice go well beyond simple steaming, occurring in a diverse range of dishes and not always recognizable as rice. In addition to being used in the production of wine and vinegar, rice grains are also converted into flour and used to make rice noodles; rice is transformed into flat rice paper sheets for wrapping *goi cuon*, the Vietnamese fresh spring rolls; glutinous rice cooked overnight, then wrapped into attractive banana leaf parcels, becomes breakfast-time *xoi* or the traditional *banh tay* and *banh chung* eaten during Tet, the Vietnamese Lunar New Year holiday (that occurs at the same time as Chinese New Year, and was adopted from the Chinese).

In the cooler northern region (conquered by the Chinese in the second century B.C.), where undulating limestone hills recall Southwest China and where many of Vietnam's ethnic groups have their homes, the cuisine shares distinct similarities with Chinese food. Stewing is a popular cooking method, and dishes rated highly in China, such as grilled dog meat and chicken feet, are great delicacies. Yet the two most famous dishes from the north are uniquely Vietnamese; both are soups eaten to fight back the winter chill. *Pho* is traditionally a breakfast dish, but can be eaten all day, and is as popular in Ho Chi Minh City as in Hanoi; *bun cha* is an aromatic dish of barbecued pork eaten in broth with noodles and herbs.

The quiet journey home from market.

In the center of the country, which is less agriculturally rich, a lack of variation in the Vietnamese diet and the demands of the reigning emperor spawned a highly developed cuisine. In the imperial city of Hue (the political capital from 1802 to 1945), the symbolic significance of food was refined to a great degree. Small portions in multiple courses, each one more beautiful than the next, elevated the food from common fare to

Right:
A bounty of fresh carrots being readied for market in Dalat, in the central highlands.
Opposite:
Smooth sailing along the tranquil waters of Halong Bay, in northern Vietnam.

chilies, coconut milk and a variety of herbs and spices.

In Dalat, just a few hours north of Ho Chi Minh City on the southern plateau, the hillsides are terraced with all sorts of western fruits and vegetables—strawberries, artichokes, oranges, mushrooms, carrots, eggplants and lettuces. The abundance of vegetables is so great that many of the region's inhabitants are vegetarians almost without thinking about it. Vast tea and coffee plantations surrounding the area could earn international attention if the quality of the harvest were improved through better handling and more sophisticated processing methods.

Heavy trucks leave Dalat every morning to deliver a bounty of fresh produce to the burgeoning markets of Ho Chi

exquisite delicacies fit for the emperor's table. Today, a delicious eggy pancake called *banh khoai* and a soup and noodle dish called *bun bo Hue* are two of Hue's best-loved streetside dishes.

In the temperate south, the cuisine more closely resembles that of neighboring Southeast Asian countries, such as Cambodia, Thailand and Malaysia. The food is more varied and rich than that of Hue or Hanoi, generously spiced with fresh

Minh City. Farther east, down the steep, winding road out toward the coastline and the South China Sea, the lowlands are blanketed with canopies of dark purple table grapes. Here several local and foreign companies have joined forces in wine-making ventures.

As investment in agriculture continues to expand throughout the country, the quality of the food produced in Vietnam will certainly improve.

What is Vietnamese Cuisine?

*A unique blend of cultural influences has created food
with its own distinct personality*

In simple terms, Vietnamese food is lighter and more refreshing than Thai food—using crisp, uncooked vegetables, subtle seasonings, raw herbs, and unique flavor combinations. Often described as textural, with fresh, sharp flavors, it is also more tropical and fragrant than Chinese food.

At the heart of Vietnamese cuisine, with its hearty kick and unique aroma, is the salty, pale brown fermented fish sauce known as *nuoc mam*. The cuisines of Cambodia, Thailand and Burma use a similar sauce, however the Vietnamese variety seems to have a more pungent flavour.

Mandatory in Vietnamese cooking, *nuoc mam* is made by layering fresh anchovies with salt in huge wooden barrels. This process takes about six months and involves pouring the liquid which drips from the barrel back over the layers of anchovies. The grading of *nuoc mam* is as sophisticated as the grading of fine olive oils. Arguably, the best *nuoc mam* comes from the island of Phu Quoc, close to the Cambodian border. A bowl of steaming rice topped with this fragrant sauce is a culinary treat in itself.

A simple, yet elegant meal in the ancient city of Hue, considered the culinary capital of Vietnam.

Nuoc mam in its purest form has a strong smell and incredibly salty flavor which renders it an acquired taste for non-Vietnamese. It is certainly stronger than Thai *nam pla* and is used in marinades and sauces, for dressing salads and in cooking. Vietnamese rarely expect a foreigner to enjoy the taste, but are delighted when one does. Easier on the unaccustomed palate is *nuoc mam cham*, which is the ubiquitous dip made of *nuoc mam* diluted with lime juice, vinegar, water, crushed garlic and fresh red chilies. *Nuoc mam cham* is used as a dipping sauce on the table, served with dishes like *cha gio* (spring rolls) and *chao tom* (sugar cane shrimps), or simply as a dip for pieces of fish or meat.

What also sets the cuisine apart from that of other Southeast Asian countries is the pervasive use of fresh leaves and herbs, which come in as many as a dozen different varieties. The use of dill in *cha ca*, Hanoi's famous fish dish served at the popular Cha Ca La Vong restaurant in the city's

Old Quarter, and also in fish congee, is likely borrowed from the French, however the extensive use of a variety of raw herbs nevertheless seems uniquely Vietnamese.

While Vietnamese restaurants in other regions of the world rarely manage to offer more than one kind of mint, basil or cilantro, markets throughout Vietnam sell a remarkable variety of herbs. Several varieties of the mint and basil family do not grow outside the country, and there are also some unusual, full-flavored leaves, like the deep-red spicy perilla leaf, *tia to*, and the pungent saw-leaf herb or long coriander that are specific to the cuisine as well.

Every *pho* shop has a huge plate of raw herbs set on each table, and a large plate also appears with an array of dishes, from grilled, marinated beef to *cha dum* (a type of pâté). But what do you do with the herbs? Sometimes, as in the case of *pho*, they are stirred into the steaming soup; with other dishes they are used as wrappers, together with rice papers or lettuces, and are featured in Vietnamese shrimp and chicken salads. The herbs are also served with *ban xeo*, a kind of crêpe enclosing shrimp, pork, mung beans and bean sprouts. Certainly the use of these fresh herbs and leafy green vegetables is part of the appeal of Vietnamese food, providing fresh flavors, beautiful aromas and many interesting textural variations.

Other factors which contribute to the subtlety and uniqueness of Vietnamese food are the refined cooking techniques, the often unusual serving of varying dishes and the combination of flavors.

Left:
One of the more visible signs of French influence.
Overleaf:
The Vietnamese countryside remains largely traditional, unaffected by the recent doi moi *economic boom in the cities.*

Imperial Cuisine

Dozens of sophisticated dishes fit for an emperor

Hue, situated on the banks of the tranquil Perfume River, is the third most visited Vietnamese city after Saigon and Hanoi. Once an important seat of learning and culture, as well as the imperial seat for nearly 150 years, it is slowly being rediscovered. This rather sleepy place is also the very city which once inspired the creation of the most sophisticated Vietnamese cuisine, and took vegetarian cuisine to even greater heights than those reached by masterful Chinese chefs.

Hue traditionally served as a cultural, educational and religious center—it is the site of the country's most important Buddhist monasteries and temples—but from 1802 to 1945 it was also the political capital of Vietnam, under the thirteen emperors of the Nguyen Dynasty. Major tourist attractions such as the Imperial Palace and the emperors' tombs still suggest a time of great affluence. Emperor Tu Duc (1848–1883), for example, whose expansive tomb reflects his once-opulent lifestyle, is said to have demanded that his morning tea be made only from the drops of water collected by his servants from lotus leaves on the lake within the Imperial City.

Emperor Tu Duc was a notoriously finicky eater, who demanded food that was markedly different from that eaten by the common person. Since Hue lacked the agricultural diversity of either the north or the south (and in those days food was not transported as routinely as it is today), the imperial kitchens were required to show an enormous amount of ingenuity—refining ordinary dishes until they became something truly special, so that eating could be viewed as art, ritual and sensory pleasure at the same time. As in China and Japan, tea-drinking was also elevated to a ceremony laden with intellectual meaning and aesthetic significance.

A typical imperial banquet today would include perhaps a dozen dishes, such as a beautifully fragrant, peppery chicken soup with lotus seeds (*sup ga*), crisp, golden brown spring rolls (*nem ran*), delicate rice flour patties stuffed with minced shrimp (*banh Hue*), grilled pork in rice paper (*thit nuong*) served with a tasty peanut sauce, delicious crab claws stuffed with pork (*cua phich bot*), and the famous minced shrimp wrapped around sugar cane (*cha tom lui mia*), known in the south as *chao tom*. Main dishes might include fish grilled in banana leaf (*ca nuong la chuoi*), pungent beef in wild betel leaves (*bo la lot*), rice with vegetables (*com Hue*), gently sautéed shrimp with mushrooms (*tom xao hanh nam*), and finally the glutinous rice dessert, which comes in a perfectly formed little box made from banana leaf. Its name literally translates as

husband-and-wife cake (*phu the*).

These dishes are actually variations of those served in other parts of Vietnam, and the ingredients may be simple vegetables, eggs or fish, rather than exotic sea delicacies or the best cuts of meat. What sets these dishes apart is the sophisticated cooking techniques and the presentation.

For example, the favorite *chao tom lui mia* seems so simple you would never guess the complexity of its preparation. The tiny shrimp are carefully shelled before marinating in *nuoc mam*. After washing, they are pounded until they form a thick paste, to which egg white, onion, garlic, sugar and pepper are added. The mixture is pounded again with a touch of pork fat, and finally wrapped around sugar cane sticks and grilled.

Appearance was very important, not only in the use of color and the arrangement of food on the plate, but also in the manner of serving. Rice, for example, might have been draped with a generous omelet coat, or cooked inside a lotus leaf and further enhanced with the addition of delicate lotus seeds. Chefs also experimented with unusual ingredients such as green banana and unripe figs, banana flowers and green corn, which until then had been considered unpalatable.

Portions were delicate, with perhaps dozens of dishes served in the course of one meal. Emperor

Tu Duc was said to order 50 different dishes every meal, prepared by 50 different cooks and served by 50 different servants. If it was possible to reduce the size of a cake or a bun, it was done. *Banh khoai*, for example, is a smaller version of the *banh xeo* so popular in the south. Even the vegetables mixed with rice are chopped into the smallest pieces possible.

All these requirements naturally increased the length of preparation time, with the result that the number of cooks and kitchen staff reached unprecedented heights—a luxury which perfectly befitted the privileged life of an emperor.

The most talented proponents of imperial cuisine today are virtually all women, each of them descended by some route or other from imperial households. Skills were painstakingly passed down in extended families, with young cooks-to-be encouraged to first observe an experienced cook before being invited to try their hand at actual preparation.

Due to its size and relatively small population, Hue today is not a culinary mecca compared with Ho Chi Minh City or Hanoi. There is, however, a renewed interest in the cuisine of Hue, and a number of modern Vietnamese chefs have made it their mission to turn the simple art of cooking into something extraordinary, and restore imperial cuisine to its former glory.

The Ascending Dragon

*Economic development sparks a burgeoning
food scene in modern Vietnam*

From the start of World War II, through the more than four troubled decades of constant struggle and fighting which followed, there was barely enough rice to go around in Vietnam, let alone interest in what to buy at the market and how to perfect a particular recipe. But since the mid-1980s, a combination of economic upturn, and the return of many overseas Vietnamese (encouraged by the government to start new businesses) has resulted in, among other things, the rebirth of a thriving restaurant scene—from flashy new establishments to informal sidewalk cafés lining the streets.

Fresh crabs are much sought-after delicacies in many Vietnamese restaurants.

Culinary skills are being relearned, courses for the training of professional chefs are being launched and, most importantly, the Vietnamese are once again discovering the joys of cooking. Top-quality, fresh ingredients are widely available. Vietnam is fortunate in being able to grow a diverse variety of vegetables and fruits throughout the country and little food is imported. Rice and seafood are once again in abundant supply.

Restaurants, which reflect this renewed interest in food, are as much about ambience—sipping a *pastis* or lingering over a bottle of fine French wine—as about the quality of food. Found all over Ho Chi Minh City and, to a slightly lesser extent, in Hanoi, these restaurants are often built around courtyards in French colonial buildings or designed to resemble old Vietnamese family homes. With their distinctly nostalgic feel, these new restaurants are not only redefining the Vietnamese aesthetic, but also serving food which is improving by the year. French restaurants are once again establishing themselves, and fashionable Italian restaurants are making an appearance, but the most interesting development is undoubtedly the new Vietnamese restaurants.

Modern Vietnamese cuisine is a marriage of the old and the new. Recipes from past generations coupled with new dishes created for the increasingly sophisticated and well-traveled local consumer. A good example is *thit kho to*, pork cooked slowly in a claypot, a dish of peasant origins which now appears on restaurant menus alongside *cua rang me*, an innovative fried crab dish, richly flavored with tamarind. The traditional Hanoi beef soup, *pho*, served with noodles, bean sprouts and fresh herbs, has gone through many transitions, but remains as tasty today as in the past.

The sometimes lengthy preparation times and cooking processes required by Vietnamese cuisine can render it something of a luxury for people with busy lives, so many chefs and teachers within Vietnam have begun experimenting with new methods that preserve the spirit of the cuisine, but allow it to be prepared quickly and simply at home. For example, deep-fried squid,

New life is being restored to many elegant French colonial buildings.

which is traditionally made with minced squid combined with egg, wrapped in rice paper and then fried, and served with lemon juice and black pepper, is today being made with whole pieces of squid to save time. The Chinese influence is also being felt. In fact, it is not unusual to find soy sauce on the table alongside *nuoc mam* in the newer restaurants.

Ironically, at the same time that this movement towards quicker cooking has been evolving, there

has also been a resurgence of interest in the traditional dishes of the Hue court, the style of Vietnamese cooking that requires the longest preparation time of all. Restaurants specializing in this cuisine often cannot open until after lunch because of the considerable amount of time required to prepare the food, and often close early at night because the food has run out.

More and more attention is being paid to

Saigon's chic new eateries cater to a growing band of discerning diners.

also be removed from the meat in the pork and bamboo shoot dish *mang ham chan goi*, though this is a move welcomed as much by health-conscious Vietnamese as by the increasing number of visitors.

The cuisine is based on rice, fish, and fresh vegetables. Little oil is used in cooking, except for deep-frying, and salads are lightly dressed. Healthy, cleansing soups such as the tasty *canh chua thom ca loc* are featured on menus, fresh fruit and delicious homemade yogurt are often served for dessert, and drinks like freshly squeezed sugar cane juice are widely available.

It seems likely that, as more cooks learn how to prepare it, and diners begin to understand and appreciate the flavors, Vietnamese food could become attractive presentation as well, although very few changes, if any, are made to cater to the tourist trade. What changes are occurring in the recipes are subtle and often imperceptible: *ga bop*, a chicken salad flavored with onion, *rau ram* herb and a simple seasoning of salt, pepper and lime juice, has traditionally been made with chicken skin and bones, but new restaurants are preparing it with lean chicken meat instead. Some fat may as popular as Chinese and Thai, which are probably the two Asian cuisines best understood and most widely available beyond their own borders. France, Australia and the United States in particular, are already key centers for Vietnamese food. However, there is nothing like eating at a smart new restaurant in a converted French villa in Ho Chi Minh City to experience the heights to which genuine Vietnamese food has risen.

Home-style Cooking

A personal approach to experiencing the essence of Vietnamese cooking

A soft rain falls as dusk approaches, as so often happens in Vietnam. The suburban streets, lined with houses and gardens, are quiet but for a few workers on their way home. Moving away from the main streets into a maze of alleys designed for motorbikes rather than cars, past the vendor selling baguettes door-to-door from a cart, we reach Tuyen's house. In the large but sparsely decorated living room, Tuyen's husband is watching television with their delightful four-year-old daughter, already in her pajamas, and their brother-in-law from the countryside. He is here visiting his eight-year-old daughter who lives with Tuyen's family in the town of Hue because he, a widower, does not earn enough money to support her. This is not unusual in Vietnam—those with higher incomes take care of those who earn less. It is a happy family scene, and they are all beginning to enjoy the smell of cooking coming from the next room.

Tuyen, slim and elegant, is chopping mushrooms and carrots into tiny cubes on a large wooden board. A talented dressmaker, by day she cuts fabric on the sturdy wooden table which takes up almost the entire room. However, tonight the table is laden with fruit, vegetables, meat and fish fresh from Hue's central market along the side of the river. A pot of gently bubbling water is on a two-ring burner. Tuyen usually cooks in the kitchen under the light of a single bulb, but she did not think that would be appropriate on this occasion.

Tonight she has promised to teach me how to cook Vietnamese food, an arrangement made by my marvelous guide Mai, who is her best friend. I arrive on the back of Mai's 50cc motorbike—a common mode of transportation—followed behind by her niece, a 19-year-old learning English at evening school, in the hope of one day becoming a tour guide. She has been commandeered to help with preparation of a very special dinner, which few would undertake during the week. Tuyen is, I am assured by Mai, the most accomplished home cook in Hue, and even then it takes even her a full morning, with two helpers, to prepare a traditionally Hue Sunday lunch.

So what do I learn? I learn that before stuffing a cabbage leaf, it it is dipped into boiling water to soften it and remove any bitterness. To soften grated carrot, it is mixed vigorously with salt and then rinsed. To extract the maximum juice from a tiny Vietnamese lime, it is rolled like a piece of dough across a hard surface before squeezing. When boiling king beans, continually remove the foam that forms at the edges of the pan. These are

Although time-consuming, the effort put into the subtle details of food preparation is the key to a rewarding culinary experience.

ter, while the remainder is mixed with just a squeeze of lime and some crushed, roasted peanuts for a wonderfully nutty-tasting salad.

I also learn that tapioca dough is nice to touch, easy to work with, and however much you knead it, it never loses its perfect smoothness—it also takes a long time to prepare. Mai, adamant that she cannot cook, spends almost the entire evening rolling the dough into little balls and stuffing flattened disks (barely larger than a coin) with steamed mung beans seasoned with salt and pepper, or coating roasted peanuts and tiny pieces of coconut in the same dough. The secret is to work with such a thin piece of dough that when each *banh bot loc* (tapioca starch cake) is cooked—about five minutes in

the types of detail Tuyen tells me everyone in Vietnam knows, but it is difficult to believe that there are many people who can carry out these tasks with the dexterity of her slim, strong, and highly competent fingers.

Mai's niece is in charge of preparing the purple banana flower, but through lack of experience cuts it the wrong way. But Tuyen does not panic; she selects some pieces for deep-frying in a wheat flour bat-

boiling water until the pieces float to the top—you achieve a translucence that means you can almost see what is inside. Once cooked, they are immediately plunged into cold water to prevent them from sticking together. Other *banh bot loc* we stuff with a single shrimp, a little pork fat and black pepper, this time forming the creations into crescent shapes, then frying them in oil with salt and a little *nuoc mam*.

Tuyen is not only a good cook, she is a good teacher as well. Her four-year-old daughter already knows how to stuff *banh bot loc*, but to play with the peanuts, rather than wrap them, is as much a temptation for this little girl as it would be for a child anywhere.

I learn how to fold rice paper in triangles around a stuffing of carrot, vermicelli noodles, and wood ear mushrooms, with a single shrimp on the top—the tail of which I am to leave sticking out at the top to give this variation on the spring roll the reason for its name, *tom phi tien*, which translates literally as flying shrimp spring roll. Unfortunately, it turns out that I am unable to wrap the rolls to Tuyen's high standards; she is concerned that if she does not re-wrap my efforts, there is a chance that the roll will disintegrate while frying.

Then Tuyan shows me how to make cabbage stuffed with carrot. I mix sugar into the softened, grated carrot, until the sugar has all but disappeared, finally adding some crushed garlic. The rolling process using cabbage is marginally easier than using rice paper, but it has to be rolled tight enough so that the rolls can be cut into colorful slices. I find the carrot slightly too sweet for my taste, but am amazed at the firm texture achieved by rolling each leaf so painstakingly tight.

Finally, I have learned how challenging and time-consuming preparing the food can be, the importance of the subtle details, and what a re-warding experience cooking genuine Vietnamese food can be.

As we sit down to dine in true Vietnamese family-style and enjoy the rewards of Tuyen's master-

Markets throughout Vietnam sell an extensive variety of fresh herbs and vegetables, which form the basis of the nation's distinctive cuisine.

ful cooking, I discover that eating in Vietnam is a shared experience, an informal ritual. On the small table that the family has gathered around is a large bowl of steaming rice, a cauldron of aromatic soup, and a generous plate of leaves that each of us wrap around a delicious hand roll and dip into the *nuoc mam cham*. Yet, as unique as this experience is to me, I realize that it is simply a typical meal for many Vietnamese families.

Part Two: The Vietnamese Kitchen

A hearth of simplicity

So central is the home and its kitchen to Vietnamese culture, that the most important time of year—Tet (the Lunar New Year)—revolves around the hearth. One week before Tet, the god of the hearth (Tao Quan) must be supplicated with a ceremony performed in the kitchen, where offerings of fruit, paper models of luxury consumer goods and a ceremonial costume, without trousers, are placed on the altar. According to folklore, the god burned his trousers by standing too close to the oven—a salutary lesson to Vietnamese cooks. The ceremony is performed to appease the god of the hearth, who is about to leave for heaven to present his annual report on the family to the Emperor of Jade, before returning home on New Year's Eve. The most important object in a Vietnamese kitchen is the altar and its resident deities.

On a more earthly level, traditional Vietnamese cooks generally squatted, feet tucked beneath them, preparing much of their food on the floor around the stove on a wet, tiled area, where all utensils, pots, pans and food items were given a cleaning before use. Even today, as incomes are gradually increasing and some of the modern conveniences (refrigerators, plumbed sinks, built-in work surfaces and electric rice cookers) are making their way into a number of Vietnamese kitchens, much of the preparation and cooking is still done in the traditional, old-fashioned way.

Most of the cooking was done over an open hearth (ovens were not used), with one member of the family on duty to fan the flames. A wok—and its accompanying utensils of bamboo or wooden spatula, sieve and brush—was, and still is, the most versatile cooking pot in any Vietnamese kitchen. Since all the cooking was done over a wood fire, grilling was the common method for cooking anything not prepared in a wok. The mortar and pestle were the most effective tools for preparing many of the necessary ingredients common to Vietnamese cuisine, and a heavy cleaver and chopping block (a smoothed board made from a tree segment was commonplace) were also essential.

In addition to the usual knives found in any kitchen, another useful implement used by the traditional cook was a narrow, two-bladed knife, used for carving vegetables into decorative shapes, and thin-slicing fruit and vegetables for the various rolls and wraps. A large pot was the standard vessel for cooking soups and stocks, and since rice has always been the staple of the Vietnamese diet, a simple rice cooker with its lid was in continual use, steaming away on a low fire.

*Opposite:
Most of the cooking is done over the open hearth in the traditional Vietnamese kitchen.*

Cooking Methods

*Tips for preparing traditional Vietnamese dishes
in a modern kitchen*

Vietnamese food, with its wide variety of textures and tastes, is surprisingly easy to cook. An entire meal can easily be prepared in a single wok or a sauté pan. While preparation has traditionally been complex and time-consuming, modern conveniences such as the food processor make the work faster and easier.

The adage "the fresher the ingredients, the better the food", is especially true of Vietnamese cooking. The various herbs and lettuces are almost always served raw, and salads are never overdressed, so that the full flavors are present. Vegetables and fish in particular, which make up a large part of the Vietnamese diet, are gently cooked and lightly seasoned, allowing the true flavors of the food to come through.

In addition to the ubiquitous and essential **fish sauce** *nuoc mam* (fortunately becoming easier to purchase outside of Vietnam), there are several key ingredients which appear in many of the recipes that require considerable preparation. Ingredients such as garlic, shallots, chili, lemongrass, roasted peanuts and ginger, that have traditionally been prepared with a mortar and pestle, can be easily managed with a food processor or a blender. However, julienne slicing is more effectively achieved with a sharp knife.

Asian **shallots** are deep-fried and used as a garnish. Alternatively, French shallots can be sliced very thinly, sprinkled lightly with salt, then gently presssed with a dry towel to dehydrate before frying.

MGS (Monosodium glutamate) is prevalent in Vietnamese food. However, due to health concerns, we have chosen to omit it from all of the recipes, which may easily be done without affecting the integrity of the food. *Nuoc mam*, salt, garlic, pepper, sugar and fried shallots—seasonings used in almost every Vietnamese dish—will compensate for its absence.

When preparing **salads**, make sure that the lettuce is fresh, cleaned and dried (use a salad spinner). Dress the salad shortly before serving, and be careful not to use too much dressing.

Dried rice papers, used to wrap a variety of rolls, can now be purchased in most Asian food markets. To prepare fresh **rice flour wrappers** (for transparent rolls), most modern cooks will have to improvise by stretching a piece of fine cloth taut over a pot of steaming water. The rice mix (rice flour, water and salt) is spooned over the surface with a large ladle and smoothed into a round pancake. After covering for a few minutes to steam through, it can be lifted up at the edges with a soft-edged utensil, removed from the cloth, and set aside to be later stuffed, rolled and sliced.

To cook **rice noodles**, use a large stock pot. Fill to a few inches from the top with water, and bring to a boil. Just before the other ingredients are ready, the noodles are placed in a large sieve, submerged for a few seconds in the boiling water, and then added to the recipe.

In general, once the ingredients have been prepared—the dicing, chopping and cutting done—they should be arranged in bowls or on a large platter, in the order they are called for in the recipe. Then, as you begin cooking, just follow the recipe and the row of pre-arranged ingredients.

The cooking methods most commonly used in Vietnamese kitchens are stir-frying, deep-frying and grilling. **Stir-fry** recipes are cooked in a wok, in either oil or pork fat over a very hot flame, for a short period of time. Sautéing in a large pan is an alternative method, although not nearly as easy. For those cooks wishing to avoid the use of pork fat (which is difficult to replace), try experimenting with other types of oil.

To stir-fry, add the oil to a preheated pan, and follow

shortly after with the ingredients that are quickly seared. Cooking generally takes only a few minutes, so that the food does not absorb too much of the oil. A traditional curved spatula or long chopsticks are best for handling the hot food.

To **deep-fry**, you can use the same wok, or a very deep saucepan since a considerable amount of oil is required (peanut oil is preferred). The optimum temperature for deep frying is between 375° and 400°F. To achieve the best results—crisp, not soggy food—cook in small amounts and maintain a high heat.

Grilling is also an important method of Vietnamese cooking that remains as popular and as practical as ever. Using a barbecue (with wood or charcoal) is one of the easiest and most effective cooking methods, since grilling over an open flame imparts very distinct and essential flavors that many of the recipes depend upon.

Vietnamese Ingredients

*Essential components for producing
authentic Vietnamese tastes and textures*

Annatto seeds

Bamboo shoots

Banana blossom

Chilies

ANNATTO SEEDS (*hot dieu do*): The dark reddish-brown seed of the "lipstick plant" is commonly used as a coloring agent. Usually seeds are fried in oil to extract a pale orange color, then discarded. Commonly available where Caribbean foods are sold.

BAMBOO SHOOTS (*mang*): Fresh, vinegared or dried (the most delicious), bamboo shoots are eaten frequently in Vietnam. Fresh shoots, which have a savory sweetness and crunchiness, should be peeled and boiled for about 30 minutes before using. Dried shoots should be soaked and boiled. Although it is difficult to find fresh shoots in the West, canned bamboo is readily available.

BANANA BLOSSOM (*bap chuoi*): This pointed pink bud, sliced finely and soaked in cold water, is used as garnish for noodle soup, and eaten raw in salads. It tastes like very tender wood shavings. Cabbage can be used as a substitute.

BANANA LEAVES (*la chuoi*): These are used primarily for wrapping cakes, sausages and pâtés. They preserve moisture, and impart a light green color and a mild flavor.

BEAN CURD SKIN (*tau hu ky*): The skin that forms on top of soybean milk when it is brought to a simmer is skimmed off and dried in thin sheets, later to be reconstituted in water. It is then deep fried, simmered or sautéed. Bean curd skin is sold fresh, frozen or dried, and is very high in protein. It is often used as a meat substitute.

BITTER MELON (*kho qua*): This hard gourd, favored for its healthful benefits, looks like a fat, knobby cucumber. Green and firm, it has a very crisp texture and a strong, bitter flavor, and is often pickled. Before cooking, the seeds and inner membrane are removed and the outer shell is sliced into small, crescent-shaped pieces.

CHAYOTE (*su hao*): A type of squash that looks like a light green cucumber, having an oval shape and a small white seed. It is also known as mirliton or christophene. A good substitute is zucchini.

CHILIES (*ot*): Many red varieties are used. Whether sliced or finely chopped, the seeds are usually removed. Dried red chilies, whole or flakes, are good substitutes.

Herbs Used In Vietnamese Cooking

Basil

BASIL *(rau que)*: Several different types of basil are used in Vietnamese cooking. The one most commonly used is similar to European and American sweet basil. It is used liberally as a seasoning and sprigs are often added to platters of fresh, raw vegetables. Similar, yet paler in color, and with a distinctive lemony fragrance, "lemon" basil is used in soups and salads.

CILANTRO *(ngo)*: Fresh cilantro—which is the leaf of the coriander plant and is often referred to as Chinese parsley—is a common garnish in Vietnamese cooking. In Vietnam, cilantro leaves are used almost exclusively as a garnish. Italian parsley can be substituted, although the flavor is not at all the same.

Cilantro

PERILLA LEAF *(la tia to)*: A wide, deep-veined, purple leaf from the mint family. It is similar to the Japanese shiso, and has a faint lemon mint flavor. Perilla leaf is part of the standard garnish, and is also used in salads and soups.

POLYGONUM *(rau ram)*: This most important of Vietnamese herbs is served

Perilla leaves

with nearly every meal. Highly aromatic, it has a pink stem and pointed, purplish leaves, which are used as a raw garnish. A combination of mint and cilantro is a good substitute. Also referred to as Vietnamese mint.

RICE PADDY HERB *(ngo om)*: Has very small, rounded, pale-green leaves that sprout at intervals along the stem, and a sharp, citrus flavor. It is used as a garnish for chicken curry and sour fish soup.

SAW-LEAF HERB *(ngo gai)*: This leaf, which smells like cilantro, is part of the standard garnish of fresh herbs that are served on the table with most Vietnamese meals. It has a long, serrated green leaf. Also called "long coriander."

WILD BETEL LEAVES *(la lot)*: The spicy and highly nutritious leaf of a vine related to the plant which produces black pepper. The large, round and crinkled leaf is used as a leafy green in soups, as an outer wrapping for spring rolls, and as part of the standard garnish. Grape leaves are a good substitute.

Polygonum

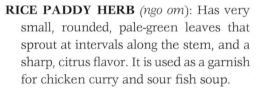

Rice paddy herb

Saw-leaf herb

Wild betel leaves

Fish sauces

Dried shrimp

Galangal

Okra

CHINESE LYCIUM (*cao ky*): A red, dried fruit available from Chinese herbalists, used in *che* and other sweet, healthy soups. Also known as boxthorn berries.

CHINESE SAUSAGES (*lap xuong*): These thin, sweet pork sausages are readily available in many countries, and a common sight on any food cart in Vietnam.

COCONUT MILK (*nuoc cot dua*): A thick coconut milk can be made for cooking by mixing grated coconut flesh with warm water, and extracting two pressings. The first pressing is rich and creamy (resembling cow's milk), and can curdle if cooked on high heat. The second pressing is much thinner and imparts far less flavor. Canned coconut milk is now widely available.

DAIKON RADISH (*cu cai trang*): Resembles a large, white carrot. Also known to the Chinese as *lobak*.

DRIED SHRIMP (*tom kho*): Widely used in cooking—in the making of shrimp sauce and as a garnish for flavor—these whole, tiny shrimp, about $1/2$ in long, are also ground into a coarse powder. Available in Asian markets.

FISH SAUCE (*nuoc mam*): The ubiquitous Vietnamese condiment used in cooking, marinades, dressings and dipping sauces, as salt or soy sauce is used in other cuisines. In its pure form, it has a very pungent, salty flavor, and is often combined with other ingredients such as sugar, garlic and lime juice to reduce its intense flavor, and to make the various dipping sauces known as *nuoc mam cham*. Use sparingly.

FIVE-SPICE POWDER (*ngu vi huong*): A Chinese spice combination of star anise, Szechuan peppercorns, fennel, cloves and cinnamon. This is a very strong seasoning and generally used in small amounts.

GALANGAL (*rieng*): A member of the ginger family, this rhizome is used in much the same way. The tough skin should always be peeled. The young, pinkish galangal is the most tender and imparts the best flavor. In certain parts of Vietnam, galangal is used as a complement for dog meat.

JACKFRUIT (*mit*): A large, green fruit with a tough, nubbly skin, which reveals a yellow, segmented flesh when opened. It has a taste that is naturally sweet. In Vietnam, the young jackfruit is used like a vegetable in cooking. Available canned in the West.

LEMONGRASS (*xa*): Also known as citronella, this intensely fragrant grass is used to impart a lemony flavor. The lower part of the stem is the edible portion. Discard the outer leaves until you reach the inner core, which should be moist and tender. When using the stalk,

VIETNAMESE NOODLES

mien

banh pho

bun

banh hoi

There are essentially four different types of noodles used in Vietnamese cooking, both fresh and dried. Glass or cellophane noodles (*mien* in the north and *bun tao* in the south) are dried, translucent noodles made from mung bean starch, which are reconstituted by pouring hot water over them. Fresh, white *pho* noodles (*banh pho*) are the wide, rice noodles used in Vietnam's classic breakfast dish, *pho*. *Bun* noodles (fresh or dried), also called rice vermicelli, are string-like in appearance and double their size, turning very white when cooked. Fine rice vermicelli noodles (*banh hoi*) are similar to *bun*, but thinner. *Mi*, dried or fresh Chinese yellow egg noodles, are used in soups and stir fries.

bruise it before cooking and discard before serving. Lemongrass is readily available fresh or frozen in many places.

Lemongrass

LOOFAH (*muop*): A type of gourd with an earthy flavor, the loofah is often used in Vietnamese soups. The insides of certain varieties are dried and used as scrubbers. Any type of gourd can be substituted.

LOTUS (*sen*): The graceful lotus bloom, often protruding from dense mud, is the symbol of purity. The tumescent root is used as a vegetable. Its seeds are used fresh (for sweet soup or *che*), or dried (in stews). The stem is stir-fried with pork or shrimp, and is also used fresh in salads.

Loofah

MUNG BEANS (*dau xanh*): When green mung beans are watered, they develop into bean sprouts. Dried green mung beans with the green skin removed are known as yellow beans. Usually soaked in water, they have a subtle flavor and a slight crunchiness. In Vietnam, yellow beans are used to make dipping sauces (yellow bean sauce) or other sauces to accompany vegetables. The starch from the beans is processed into cellophane noodles.

Lotus stems

MUSHROOMS (*nam*): Delicate straw mushrooms are the most commonly used fresh varieties. Wood or tree ear are the most commonly used dried mushrooms—they have a crunchy texture and very little flavor, but make

Mung bean sprouts

Pomelo

Rice paper

Sesame rice crackers

Shrimp crackers

a fine filling. Other dried varieties are similar to the Chinese and Japanese, such as the shiitake (also known as dried black) mushrooms.

OKRA (*dau bap*): A green, five-sided vegetable favored by Indians and Southeast Asians. Also known as lady's finger.

OYSTER SAUCE (*dau hau*): A thick sauce made from ground oysters, water, salt, cornstarch and caramel coloring, used primarily for stir-frying vegetables. It is more commonly used in Chinese than in Vietnamese cooking.

PALM SUGAR (*duong the*): A type of sugar made by boiling down the sap of various palm trees. It is used as a sweetener and also to help balance saltiness in savory dishes. If unavailable, you can make your own caramelized sugar (adding a touch of maple syrup), as a reasonable substitute.

POMELO (*buoi*): The Vietnamese equivalent to grapefruit, the pomelo is drier, sweeter, has a much thicker and tougher peel. It is usually eaten dipped in a chili mix, or crumbled and served in salads. It is increasingly available in the West.

RICE PAPER (*banh trang*): Made from a batter of rice flour, water and salt, the paper is steamed and dried in the sun on bamboo racks, which leaves a crosshatched imprint. Used to wrap a wide variety of rolls, the paper

must be moistened with a wet cloth before using, to allow greater flexibility. Available in many Asian food markets.

SAGO PEARLS (*bot bang*): The pith of the sago palm is ground into a paste that is very glutinous, but has little taste. Sago pearls are used in Vietnam to make desserts.

SESAME RICE CRACKERS (*banh trang me*): These are thin crackers made from rice flour, sprinkled with sesame seeds. They must be grilled or lightly baked before serving and are used like a cracker for dipping. Shrimp crackers or puffed rice crackers may be used as a substitute.

SHRIMP CRACKERS (*banh phong tom*): Also called shrimp chips, these light, crisp crackers are made from finely ground shrimp, tapioca starch, and egg whites pressed together and dried. When fried in hot oil, they expand into light, crispy crackers that dissolve in your mouth, leaving a mild shrimp taste. Very popular in Vietnam, particularly during Tet, they are often served as a snack with a dipping sauce, or as an accompaniment to a main course.

SHRIMP PASTE (*mam ruoc*): A dense mixture of fermented, ground shrimp found in markets throughout Vietnam and other countries in Southeast Asia—piled in large, dark brown or muddy red mounds. It is used in small amounts, due to its strong flavor.

STAR ANISE (*hoi*): A star-shaped, eight-pointed pod from the flower of an evergreen tree grown in northern Vietnam, star anise has a pungent flavor of aniseed or licorice. Used most often in soups (*pho*, in particular) or other recipes requiring long simmering.

STARFRUIT (*khe*): Eaten raw and finely sliced, the young starfruit has a tart taste, and is often served on the Vietnamese vegetable platter along with unripe, sliced bananas. Delicious with grilled or fried foods

SUGAR CANE (*mia*): Fresh sugar cane juice—the green liquid extracted from the stalks by a crushing machine—is a very popular drink in Vietnam. In addition to the familiar uses of sugar cane, the peeled stalks are also used as skewers in cooking.

TAMARIND (*me*): A large, brown pod with several seeds that is rich in vitamins. Tamarind has a tangy, acidic taste, and is one of the more popular sour flavorings throughout the world. It can be bought fresh, dried, or in pulp form, and is most commonly sold in compressed blocks, with the seeds removed. The paste is used in hot and sour soups, and fresh crab dishes.

TAPIOCA STARCH (*bot nang*): This starch from the cassava root (*khoai mi*) is used as a thickening agent, and sometimes in the making of fresh rice papers. Combined with rice flour, it adds a translucent sheen and chewiness to pastries. Available in many Asian food markets.

TARO (*khoai mon* or *khoaiso*): A barrel-shaped oval root, with hairy, brown skin and white flesh with purple/brown fibers, best eaten when these fibers are small and barely noticeable. Can be used as potato in soups. Cook at least 15 minutes, until soft and creamy.

TURMERIC (*nghe*): A bright yellow-orange tuber from the same family as ginger and galangal, with a more subtle flavor. Turmeric is used often in curries and as a coloring agent. It is also used for medicinal purposes and can be applied to wounds to diminish scarring.

WATER SPINACH (*rau muong*): Also referred to as morning glory or water convolvulus. Water spinach, with its arrowhead-shaped leaves and long, hollow stem, grows in swamps. Both the leaves and a portion of the stems are used. Not readily available.

Star anise

Tamarind

Turmeric

Daikon radish

Part Three: The Recipes

Recipes for pickles, dipping sauces and stocks
precede those for the main dishes, which begin on page 40

PRESERVED AND PICKLED VEGETABLES

Do Thua • *Preserved Mixed Vegetables*

1 medium daikon radish, finely sliced
Salt
10 shallots, finely sliced
1 medium carrot, finely sliced
1 cup finely sliced chayote or green papaya
2 cups fish sauce
$\frac{1}{2}$ cup palm sugar
2 or 3 small red chilies, seeded and sliced
2 cloves garlic, finely chopped
1 teaspoon salt
2 teaspoons pepper

Sprinkle radish with salt and let sit for 30 minutes. Pat dry with a towel. Wash and dry the shallots. Dry all the vegetables in the sun for 1 day (or in a very low-temperature oven, for approximately 3 hours). Place in a sterilized glass jar. In a small saucepan, heat fish sauce, palm sugar, chilies, garlic, salt and pepper. Simmer and reduce for 10 minutes, or until reduced by one-third. Pour liquid into jar. Close the lid. Marinate for 1 week.

Helpful hint: To sterilize glass jars, wash thoroughly in soapy water. Bring to a boil in water to cover, and boil for 10 minutes.

Time Estimates

Time estimates are for preparation only (excluding cooking) and are based on the assumption that a food processor or blender will be used.

🕐 *quick and very easy to prepare*

🕐🕐 *relatively easy; less than 15 minutes' preparation*

🕐🕐🕐 *takes more than 15 minutes to prepare*

Opposite, left:
Pickled Shrimp (no recipe), Mustard Greens, and Pig's Ear.
Opposite, right:
Pickled Green Onions, Water Spinach, Lotus Root, Baby Pickles, and Mixed Vegetables.

Cai Chua • *Preserved Mustard Greens*

1 pound mustard greens
2 cups water
1 tablespoon salt
$^1/_4$ cup sugar

Dry mustard greens in the sun for half a day (or in a very low-temperature oven for $1^1/_2$ hours) or until semi-dry. Blanch in boiling salted water for 1 minute and drain. Cut into short segments, or keep in whole pieces. Place in a sterilised glass jar. Bring water, salt and sugar to a boil, then cool down. Pour the liquid into the jar, making sure that all leaves are covered. Marinate for 1 week, or until the stems turn yellow and crisp.

Cu Kieu • *Pickled Spring Onions*

1 pound spring onions, white part only
2 cups vinegar
$^1/_2$ cup palm sugar
2 tablespoons salt

Below: An assortment of pickles. From left to right: baby cucumbers, shrimp, mixed variety, baby leek tips, and pig's ear.

Dry the onions under the sun, for half a day (or in a very low-temperature oven, for $1^1/_2$ hours) or until semi-dry. Boil the vinegar, sugar and salt; allow to cool. Pour liquid into the jar to cover the onions. Marinate for 3 days. Will last for 2–3 weeks refrigerated.

Dua Gia • *Pickled Bean Sprouts*

1 cup bean sprouts
1 bunch chives, cut into $1^1/_2$-inch lengths
2 cups cold water
2 tablespoons salt

Soak the bean sprouts and chives in the cold, salted water for 1 day. Keep in the refrigerator. Drain before serving. Strips of carrot can also be added.

Ca Rot • *Carrot and Radish Pickles*

1 cup julienned carrot
1 cup julienned daikon radish
1 tablespoon salt
2 tablespoons sugar
$^1/_4$ cup white vinegar

Sprinkle carrot and radish with salt, allow to stand for 10 minutes. Press vegetables gently with a dry towel to remove excess moisture. Rinse and drain. In a mixing bowl, combine sugar and vinegar with vegetables, then marinate for at least 2 hours before serving. Best when served chilled.

Bap Cai Muoi Xoi • *Preserved Cabbage*

1 medium cabbage, diced
1 tablespoon salt
1 tablespoon crushed ginger root
2 cups vinegar
2 tablespoons sugar
2 tablespoons finely chopped *rau ram* (polygonum leaves)

Sprinkle the cabbage with salt and ginger, and allow to stand for 30 minutes. With a dry towel, press the excess moisture from the cabbage (a salad spinner works well here). Place cabbage in a jar. Mix vinegar, sugar and *rau ram*, and pour over the cabbage until completely covered. After 1 day, as the cabbage begins to ferment, bubbles will appear. When the liquid in the jar is clear and the bubbles are gone (roughly 3 days later), it is ready to eat.

DIPPING SAUCES & CONDIMENTS

Nuoc Mam Cham • *Fish Sauce Dip*

$\frac{1}{4}$ cup water or fresh coconut juice
1 teaspoon rice vinegar
1 teaspoon sugar
1 red chili, seeded, finely chopped
2 cloves garlic, crushed
1 tablespoon lime juice
2 tablespoons fish sauce

Boil water or coconut juice with vinegar and sugar; allow to cool. Combine chili, garlic, and lime juice, and add to the coconut mixture. Stir in the fish sauce.

Try adding shredded radish and carrot pickles as a variation on *nuoc mam cham*.

Mam Nem • *Fermented Anchovy Dip*

2 tablespoons fermented anchovy sauce or paste
$\frac{1}{2}$ cup water
2 teaspoons vinegar
2 tablespoons crushed pineapple
$\frac{1}{4}$ stalk lemongrass, finely chopped
1 red chili, finely chopped
1 clove garlic, crushed
1 teaspoon sugar
Pinch of pepper

Combine all the ingredients and stir well. Season to taste with pepper and sugar.

Above: Salt and Chili Dipping Sauce.

Nuoc Tuong • *Yellow Bean Sauce*

1 cup yellow beans, boiled and drained
2 tablespoons coconut milk
2 tablespoons ground peanuts
2 teaspoons sugar
3 cloves garlic
1 medium red chili
1 stalk lemongrass
2 tablespoons vegetable oil

Combine all ingredients, except oil, in a food processor. Blend until finely chopped and well combined. Heat oil in pan, stir-fry all ingredients and simmer for 2 minutes. Cool before serving.

Sot Dau Phong • *Peanut Sauce*

1 clove garlic, finely sliced
2 teaspoons vegetable oil
4 ounces pork or chicken liver
1 tablespoon finely chopped red chili
$\frac{1}{2}$ cup Yellow Bean Sauce (see previous recipe)
1 stem lemongrass, finely chopped
$\frac{1}{4}$ cup coconut milk
1 teaspoon sugar

1 teaspoon salt
2 tablespoons tamarind juice
1 cup finely ground peanuts

Sauté garlic in oil until soft, add liver, chili, yellow bean sauce, lemongrass, half the coconut milk, sugar, salt, tamarind juice and peanuts. Bring to a boil. Remove from heat. Blend in a food processor, add remaining coconut milk.

Nuoc Tuong Toi Ot • *Soy Sauce Dip*

¹/₄ cup soy sauce
1 clove garlic, finely chopped
1 teaspoon sugar
1 teaspoon pepper
1 medium red chili, finely chopped
1 lime, cut into wedges and squeezed

Combine all ingredients and mix well. Add a squeeze of fresh lime to taste.

Sot Ca Chua • *Tomato Sauce*

1 tablespoon vegetable oil
3 cloves garlic, finely chopped
3 medium tomatoes, peeled, seeded and finely chopped
1 cup chicken stock or fresh coconut juice
Pinch of salt
1 teaspoon sugar

Heat oil and sauté garlic until slightly browned. Add tomatoes, then stir for 5 minutes, adding stock or coconut juice. Bring the combination to a boil, add a small amount of water. Mix thoroughly, reduce heat, then season to taste with salt and sugar. Simmer until reduced by one-third or until desired thickness is achieved.

Sot Chua Ngot • *Sweet and Sour Sauce*

3 cloves garlic, finely chopped
1 tablespoon oil
2 tablespoons sliced shallots
2 pickled shallots, sliced
1 small carrot, diced
1 small green bell pepper, diced
1 medium red chili, diced
1 tablespoon sugar
Salt, pepper
1 teaspoon Tomato Sauce (see previous recipe)
2 tablespoons vinegar
1 tablespoon cornstarch mixed with a teaspoon of water

Sauté garlic in oil until slightly colored. Add sliced shallots, pickled shallots, carrot, green bell pepper, chili, sugar, and salt and pepper to taste. Keep frying, add tomato sauce and vinegar. Bring combination to a boil, add cornstarch mixture. Reduce heat, stir and simmer for 1 minute.

Nuoc Mau • *Caramel Syrup*

1 cup water
1 cup brown sugar

Bring water and sugar to a boil. Stir and reduce until liquid is a dark brown color. Remove

Above: Peanut Sauce (top) and fish sauce with garlic and chilies (bottom).
Below Right: The classic Vietnamese garnish platter including fish sauce, fragrant leaves, chilies and limes.

from heat, add a few tablespoons of water and stir. Pour into a heatproof container. Cover with a lid.

Muoi Tieu Chanh •
Salt, Pepper and Lime Mix

1 teaspoon salt
1 teaspoon pepper
$1/2$ lime

Combine salt and pepper, squeeze lime juice into the mixture and stir well.

STOCKS

Nuoc Leo Ga • *Chicken Stock*

3 quarts water
3-pound chicken
1 tablespoon whole white peppercorns
1 cup sliced onions
1 medium carrot, chopped
1 stalk celery, chopped
Pinch of salt
Pinch of pepper

Combine the ingredients in a large stock pot; bring to a boil. Simmer for 2–3 hours, until stock is reduced by half, strain and set aside. Once cool, remove solid fat residue layer off the top.

Helpful hint: Use cooked chicken for other recipes.

Nuoc Leo Bo • *Beef Stock*

4 quarts water
$4^1/2$ pounds beef bones
2 tablespoons sliced ginger root
2 pieces star anise
Pinch of salt and pepper

Combine all ingredients, bring to a boil and simmer for 3 hours. Strain and set aside. Once cool, remove solid fat residue off the top.

Nuoc Leo Rau Cai • *Vegetable Stock*

4 quarts water
1 cup sliced carrots
1 cup sliced cabbage
$1/2$ cup sliced celery
$1/4$ cup sliced daikon radish
1 tablespoon salt
1 tablespoon pepper

Combine all the ingredients and boil for 1 hour or until the liquid is reduced by a half. Strain and set aside.

Helpful hint: Stocks should be placed in sealed containers and refrigerated, or frozen if they are to be stored for a longer time. Refrigerated stock will last for 1 week.

Below: Fish Sauce Dip with shredded carrot (top) and chili sauce (bottom).

BI CUON & GOI CUON

Pork Roll & Shrimp Roll

BI CUON ①②③

4 ounces pork skin
1 cup water
2 teaspoons brown sugar
1 teaspoon rice vinegar
1 pound pork loin, sliced
1 cup coconut juice
2 tablespoons vegetable oil
2 cloves garlic, crushed
Salt
Pepper
20 pieces dried rice paper
1 medium head butter lettuce
1 cup fresh basil leaves
1 cup fresh mint leaves

Opposite: Shrimp Roll (top), Pork Roll (bottom) with fish sauce and peanut sauce.

Roll pork skin and tie with a string. In a saucepan, bring water to a boil. Add pork skin. Simmer for 8–10 minutes or until well cooked, drain. Cool and slice very thinly. Add sugar and vinegar. Set aside.

Place sliced pork loin in saucepan with coconut juice, simmer over medium heat until half cooked. In a separate pan, heat oil over medium heat and add garlic. Cook until lightly browned, then add pork loin and sauté until well done. Remove from heat, cool down and shred into thin pieces.

Combine pork skin, pork, salt and pepper.

Rub rice paper with a moist towel until paper is soft and flexible. Place a little of the lettuce, basil, mint and pork mixture on the paper. Roll up firmly. Cut into finger-length (3-inch to 4-inch) pieces.

Serve with Fish Sauce Dip (page 37).

GOI CUON ①②③

$\frac{1}{2}$ cup water
2 tablespoons white vinegar
1 tablespoon rice wine
$\frac{1}{2}$ teaspoon salt
1 pound shrimp, with shells on
2 tablespoons vegetable oil
8 ounces pork loin
20 pieces dried rice paper
1 medium head butter lettuce
1 cup fresh basil leaves
1 cup fresh mint leaves
2 small red chilies, thinly sliced
1 cup bean sprouts
1 bunch chives, cut in 3-inch to 4-inch lengths

In a frying pan, combine water, vinegar, rice wine and salt. Bring to a boil. Add shrimp, simmer until just done. Cool and peel. Heat oil in a separate pan, sear pork in pan for about 2 minutes or until lightly browned all over. Add liquid from cooking shrimp to the pan, simmer pork for 15 minutes or until tender. Remove from heat, drain and cut into thin slices. Follow the same steps as for wrapping the pork roll using lettuce, basil, mint, chilies, bean sprouts and chives. Serve with Peanut Sauce (page 37).

BANH UOT THIT NUONG & CUON HUE

Grilled Beef Roll & Hue Spring Roll

BANH UOT THIT NUONG ☻☻

1 stem lemongrass, finely chopped
1 tablespoon soft brown sugar
$\frac{1}{4}$ cup fish sauce
12 ounces beef, thinly sliced
5 fresh steamed rice flour wrappers
  (see page 44)
$\frac{1}{2}$ cup fresh mint leaves
$\frac{1}{2}$ cup fresh basil leaves
$\frac{1}{2}$ head butter lettuce
1 tablespoon sesame seeds, toasted
$\frac{1}{2}$ cup fresh cilantro leaves

Combine lemongrass, sugar and fish sauce. Marinate beef in sauce mixture for 30 minutes, then briefly grill over a medium heat until lightly browned, but still rare inside. Remove from grill and cut into small pieces. Place some of the beef, a little of the mint, basil and lettuce leaves on a rice flour wrapper, then sprinkle with sesame seeds and add a cilantro leaf. Fold to the inside, leaving the top end open with the cilantro leaf extended.

Dipping Sauce:

1 cup Yellow Bean Sauce (see page 37)
4 tablespoons sweet chili sauce
1 tablespoon finely chopped roasted peanuts

Combine Yellow Bean Sauce, chili sauce and peanuts. Mix well.

CUON HUE ☻☻

5 fresh steamed rice flour wrappers
  (see page 44)
1 large rice paper, sprinkled with water
8 sprigs water spinach
$\frac{1}{2}$ cup fresh fragrant leaves (mixture of basil, mint and cilantro)
1 medium sweet potato, peeled, cooked and thinly sliced
$\frac{1}{4}$ cup steamed rice vermicelli noodles
4 ounces lean pork, boiled and thinly sliced
4 ounces preserved sour shrimp

Spread steamed rice flour wrappers over softened rice paper (which makes it easier to roll but is discarded). Place water spinach, fragrant leaves, sweet potato and rice noodles in a line along the paper. Roll tightly. Cut into 1-inch segments and display them on a plate, topping each segment with a slice of pork and a shrimp. Serve with shrimp paste dip.

Shrimp Paste Dip:

2 cloves garlic, finely chopped
2 tablespoons vegetable oil
1 tablespoon shrimp paste
1 sweet potato, boiled and mashed
1 tablespoon sugar

Sauté garlic in oil until fragrant. Add shrimp paste, potato and sugar. Stir well, cook for a few minutes.

BANH CUON

Stuffed Steamed Rice Wrapper Rolls

This is where a little kitchen ingenuity helps. The steaming of the fresh rice flour wrappers is actually quite easy and fun, once you master the method.

This is another variation on the spring roll, using freshly steamed wrappers. ☺☺☺

Stuffing:
½ cup dried wood ear mushrooms
Water to cover
2 tablespoons vegetable oil
8 shallots, chopped
1 clove garlic, crushed
1 cup finely diced preserved white radish
10 ounce ground pork or minced shrimp

Fresh Rice Flour Wrappers:
1 cup rice flour
3 cups water
Salt

Garnish:
¼ cup cilantro leaves
½ cup fried shallots
1 red chili, shredded

Sauce:
1 tablespoon sugar
¼ cup water
2 tablespoons fish sauce
1 tablespoon rice wine vinegar
1 tablespoon fresh lime juice

1 medium red chili, shredded
2 cloves garlic, finely chopped

Stuffing: Soak the wooden ear mushrooms in water for 1 hour, drain and dice. Heat oil in a wok and sauté the shallots, garlic, radish, pork and mushrooms until tender. Set aside.

Wrappers: Mix flour, water and salt to form the batter. Fill steamer two-thirds full of water, double and stretch a piece of cheesecloth tightly over the top and secure it with string. When water begins boiling, brush the surface of the cheesecloth with oil, pour on a small ladle of rice flour batter and spread it around in a circular motion. If possible, cover with an inverted bowl or lid, and leave for a few moments. Remove the steamed rice flour wrapper with a spatula, carefully lifting up at the corners. Repeat until all the batter is used. Set the wrapper on a smooth surface. Place roughly 1 tablespoon of filling on the wrapper. Roll up gently. **Garnish** with cilantro, shallots and chili.

Sauce: Dissolve sugar in water, add fish sauce, vinegar and lime juice. Add finely chopped chili and garlic before serving.

CHA GIO

Vietnamese Spring Rolls

These are the classic, deep-fried Vietnamese spring rolls, also referred to as Imperial Rolls. ☺☺☺

Stuffing:

- 1 pound leanground pork
- 8 ounces peeled shrimp, minced
- 4 ounces crabmeat
- 5 shallots, finely chopped
- 2 cloves garlic, crushed
- 2 or 3 wood ear mushrooms, soaked in water
- 1½ ounces cellophane noodles, soaked in water
- ½ medium carrot, cut in julienne shreds
- 1 egg white (optional)
- Pinch pepper
- 1 teaspoon sugar
- Pinch salt
- 1 tablespoon fish sauce

In a large bowl, combine the stuffing ingredients; mix thoroughly.

Wrapping:

- 25 pieces dried rice paper
- Water
- Vegetable oil for deep-frying

Opposite: Vietnamese Spring Rolls with Fish Sauce Dip, fragrant leaves and bean sprouts.

Cover rice paper with banana leaf or sprinkle with water until flexible. Put a heaped teaspoon of stuffing on the rice paper. Start folding the left and right side of the rice paper into the center, then roll up from the bottom edge away to the far end. Do not roll too tight, as this will cause the rolls to split. Deep-fry over medium heat until golden brown.

Garnish:

- 1 cup fragrant leaves (basil, cilantro and mint)
- 1 small head iceberg lettuce
- ¼ cup bean sprouts
- 2 tablespoons Fish Sauce Dip (see page 37)
- 2 tablespoons Carrot and Radish Pickles (see page 36)
- ½ cup rice noodles, softened

Serve with fragrant leaves, lettuce, bean sprouts, Fish Sauce Dip, Carrot and Radish Pickles and fine rice noodles.

Helpful hints: The leaves and the lettuce are wrapped around the rolls and then dipped into the sauce. This is a fun recipe to experiment with. Try using different ingredients, such as chicken or duck.

CHAO TOM & THIT CHUNG TRUNG

Shrimp Mousse on Sugar Cane & Vietnamese Egg Cakes

CHAO TOM

This is a very important Vietnamese dish, from the imperial capital of Hue. It uses fresh sticks of sugar cane as skewers. The heated cane releases a burst of sweet cane juice when bitten into. ☯ ☯ ☯

> 10 ounces ($1^1/_4$ cups) shrimp, minced
> $^1/_2$ teaspoon salt
> 1 teaspoon sugar
> Pinch of pepper
> 2 tablespoons vegetable oil
> 8 sugar cane pieces, 4 inches long
> 1 red chili, seeded and sliced
> 1 cup Sweet and Sour Sauce (see page 38)
> $^1/_2$ cup cilantro leaves

Opposite: Shrimp Mousse on Sugar Cane (right), and Vietnamese Egg Cake (left) with Sweet and Sour Sauce, and chili and soy sauce.

Grind or pound shrimp with salt, sugar and pepper. Using the oil, form the shrimp paste around the sugar cane until tight. Grill over medium charcoal heat until crisp and slightly browned.

Serve with chili, Sweet and Sour Sauce and cilantro leaves.

Helpful hints: Although the pounding is normally done in a mortar, you can use a blender or a food processor. Crab is a good substitute for shrimp. If grilling is not possible, oven bake at 375°F for about 20 minutes.

THIT CHUNG TRUNG

This is a hearty, home-style dish that can be served for breakfast, lunch or dinner. ☯ ☯ ☯

> $1^1/_2$ ounces cellophane noodles
> Boiling water
> 2 dried wood ear mushrooms
> 3 cloves garlic, minced
> 1 tablespoon vegetable oil
> 6 eggs
> 12 ounces ground pork
> $^1/_2$ teaspoon salt
> Pinch of pepper
> 1 teaspoon sugar
> $^1/_2$ cup cilantro leaves
> 2 red chilies, sliced
> $^1/_4$ cup soy sauce

Soak noodles in water to soften. Drain and cut into $^1/_2$-inch segments. Soak mushrooms in water for 10 minutes, drain and cut into narrow strips.

Cook garlic in oil until soft and lightly browned. Beat eggs, add garlic, pork, noodles, mushrooms and season with salt, pepper and sugar. Mix well, pour mixture into small bowls (or one large bowl), set in a pan with a little water, cover and steam in a pre-heated oven, at 300°F, for about 30 minutes.

Vietnamese egg cakes are served with steamed rice, cilantro, chili and soy sauce.

BANH KHOAI

Hue Pancake

The Vietnamese version of an open-faced omelet or crêpe, this specialty of many streetside restaurants is also called the "Happy Pancake." The Vietnamese name, *khoai*, comes from the type of pan it is cooked in. *Banh xeo* is the large southern version. 🕐🕐🕐

1 cup rice flour
1½ cups water
1 teaspoon superfine sugar
2 tablespoons cooking oil
4 ounces peeled shrimp (small)
3 strips of thinly sliced cooked lean pork or bacon
½ cup finely sliced straw mushrooms
½ cup bean sprouts
2 eggs, beaten
Salt
Pepper
1 cup fragrant leaves (basil, cilantro and mint)
2 medium starfruit, sliced
1 cup Soy Sauce Dip (see page 38)

Blend rice flour with water and sugar, leave to rest for 10 minutes then strain.

Heat oil in a large frying pan, add shrimp and pork or bacon. Sauté for 2–3 minutes, or until lightly browned. Ladle rice flour mix into pan. Add mushrooms and bean sprouts. Cook, covered, for 1 minute. Stir eggs into mixture and cook, covered again, for about 3 minutes or until browned and crispy. Season with salt and pepper.

Remove and assemble on a serving plate. Serve with fragrant leaves, starfruit and Soy Sauce Dip.

Helpful hint: Ideally, this dish should be prepared over a very high heat (to crisp the pancake), in a non stick pan.

CHA LUA & NEM CHUA

Pork Sausage & Pickled Sour Pork Sausage

CHA LUA

Two very different versions of pork sausage found in any Vietnamese charcuterie. ◷◷◷

1 pound pork loin
8 ounces meat from small pig's head
2 cups salted water
¼ cup cooking oil
5 shallots, diced
2 cloves garlic, crushed
½ cup wood ear mushrooms, finely chopped
3 tablespoons whole black peppercorns
¼ cup sesame seeds, toasted
2 eggs, beaten
1 large banana leaf
3 tablespoons fish sauce
2 limes, cut into wedges

Opposite:
*A "charcuterie"
of Vietnamese
sausage (top of
plate) and Pork
Sausage (bottom
of plate).*

Boil pork and pig's head in salted water for 20 minutes, drain and de-bone; cut into small cubes. Heat oil in a large frying pan, cook shallots and garlic until soft. Add pork, mushrooms and peppercorns. Cook, stirring until mushrooms are soft; finish with sesame seeds. Remove from heat, stir eggs through pork mixture.

Place mixture on the banana leaf, wrap and tie with a string. Steam for 2 hours (above boiling water). Unwrap and slice thinly. Serve with fish sauce and lime wedges.

NEM CHUA ◷◷◷

1 pound pork loin, sliced
1 teaspoon salt
2 teaspoons sugar
¼ cup fish sauce
4 ounces pork skin
3 cloves garlic, crushed
2 tablespoons vegetable oil
½ cup uncooked rice, roasted and ground
Banana leaves
2 cloves garlic, sliced
1 small red chili, sliced
½ cup Pickled Baby Leeks (see page 36)

Pound pork meat thin and marinate with a portion of the salt, sugar and fish sauce. Cook pork skin until golden; allow to cool and cut into fine strips. Gently sauté the garlic in oil until fragrant, then add remaining fish sauce and sugar, and reduce to a thick consistency.

Combine pork meat, pork skin, garlic, fish sauce and the rice meal. Shape into patties and place on banana leaf. Add a slice of garlic and a slice of chili before wrapping the "sausage" in the leaf. Refrigerate for 2 days. Serve with pickled leeks.

GOI NGO SEN

Lotus Stem Salad with Shrimp

The lotus flower is the symbol of purity. The stems make a delicious salad, as they have a crisp, crunchy texture similar to celery (which can be used as a substitute). ☺☺☺

8 ounces cleaned lotus stems, cut into 2-inch lengths
1 tablespoon finely chopped *rau ram* (polygonum) leaves
1 teaspoon salt
$1\frac{1}{2}$ tablespoons sugar
1 tablespoon lime juice
6 medium shrimp, cooked, peeled, deveined
1 tablespoon coarsely ground peanuts
3 tablespoons cilantro leaves
2 tablespoons fried shallots
$\frac{1}{3}$ cup Fish Sauce Dip (see page 37)
6 shrimp crackers

In a large bowl, combine lotus stems, *rau ram* leaves, salt, sugar and lime juice; toss gently. Place on a serving plate. Cut shrimp in half lengthwise and arrange on the salad. Garnish with ground peanuts, cilantro leaves and fried shallots. Serve with Fish Sauce Dip and shrimp crackers.

Helpful hint: Most Vietnamese salads are quickly and easily assembled once the preparation is done, often requiring nothing more than a light toss with a small amount of dressing just before serving.

GOI MUC

Squid Salad

Squid is a versatile sea creature featured in many recipes. Once cleaned, it is surprisingly easy to work with. ☉☉☉

1 pound cleaned squid
4 cups water
2 tablespoons lime juice
¼ cup rice wine
3 cloves garlic, crushed
1 teaspoon sesame oil
1 teaspoon sugar
1 teaspoon cracked black pepper
½ cup thinly sliced baby celery
½ cup cilantro leaves
1 small red chili, finely chopped
⅓ cup Pickled Baby Leeks (see page 36) or shallots (optional)
2 tablespoons crushed peanuts
¼ cup Fish Sauce Dip (see page 37)
Rice Crackers, to garnish

Cut squid crosswise, in narrow sections, about 2 inches long. Bring large pan of water to a boil and blanch squid quickly (1–2 minutes). Cool down in ice water, to preserve soft texture.

Combine remaining ingredients with the squid. Mix well in a large bowl. Arrange on a platter. Serve with rice crackers.

Helpful hint: Squid becomes rubbery if overcooked. The secret to making this an appetizing dish is to barely cook the squid and quickly plunge it in ice water so it has a soft, velvety texture. In Vietnam, as elsewhere in Asia, the squid is crisscrossed with tiny cuts before cooking to achieve decorative patterns. Squid can also be tenderized by soaking it in milk for a day before cooking.

GOI MIT TRON

Jackfruit Salad

A texturally pleasing recipe that calls for young un-ripe jackfruit—different from the sweeter, mature fruit. Young jackfruit resemble a vegetable, with a firm texture and a mild flavor. Cabbage can be used as a substitute. 🕐🕐🕐

2 cloves garlic, crushed
2 tablespoons vegetable oil
4 large shrimp, peeled
2 ounces lean pork, sliced
Pinch pepper
$^1/_3$ teaspoon salt
$^1/_2$ teaspoon sugar
8 ounces young jackfruit, boiled and thinly
    sliced
1 teaspoon chopped *rau ram* (polygonum)
    leaves
1 teaspoon sesame seeds, toasted
Sesame seed rice crackers

Sauté garlic in oil until fragrant. Add shrimp, pork, pepper, salt and sugar. Stir until shrimp and pork are cooked, then add jackfruit and mix well. Add *rau ram* leaves and half of the sesame seeds. Mix well again. Arrange on plate. Sprinkle remaining sesame seeds over the salad. Serve with sesame seed rice crackers.

Helpful hints: This salad is at its best when served slightly warm. Try scooping up the salad with the rice crackers for a unique combination of flavors.

GOI XOAI XANH TOM HAP & GOI BUOI

Shrimp and Green Mango Salad & Pomelo Salad

GOI XOAI TOM NUONG ☺☺☺

This is essentially a variation on the traditional Vietnamese shrimp salad—using tart, unripe mango instead of lotus root. Green papaya may also be used.

- 12 medium shrimp
- 1 cup finely sliced green mango
- 1 tablespoon chopped *rau ram* (polygonum) leaves
- 1/4 cup Fish Sauce Dip (see page 37)

Garnish:

- 1 small red chili, finely sliced
- 2 tablespoons fried shallots
- 2 tablespoons chives

Opposite: *Shrimp and Green Mango Salad (left) and Pomelo Salad (right).*

Peel and devein the shrimp. Quickly steam in a pan with very little water until bright pink and tender. Remove from pan and cool. In a large bowl, combine the shrimp, mango, *rau ram* and Fish Sauce Dip. Toss well. Arrange on a platter. Top with garnish.

GOI BUOI ☺☺☺

This is a relatively new creation, employing the deliciously sweet Vietnamese pomelo, which is similar to grapefruit, but not as sour.

- 1/2 cup crabmeat
- 1/2 cup cooked and cubed chicken breast
- 1/2 cup julienned carrot
- 1/4 cup sliced cucumber
- 1 medium pomelo, peeled and crumbled
- 1/4 cup Fish Sauce Dip (see page 37)
- 1 tablespoon finely chopped mint leaves
- 2 tablespoons coarsely ground peanuts
- 1 tablespoon finely chopped cilantro
- 1 tablespoon fried shallots

Combine all the ingredients except peanuts, cilantro and shallots. Toss gently in a large mixing bowl. Serve slightly chilled, garnished with peanuts, cilantro and shallots.

Helpful hints: Grapefruit can be substituted for pomelo, but should be used more sparingly since it is more sour and bitter. Since fish sauce (and the various dipping sauces it makes) has such presence, it's always a good idea to adjust the amounts used in the recipes to suit the flavor of a particular dish.

GOI GA BAP CAI & NAM XAO NUOC TUONG

Cabbage Salad with Chicken & Braised Mushrooms with Soy Sauce

GOI GA BAP CAI

This is the classic chicken salad found in most restaurants throughout Vietnam. The unique mixture of textures and flavors makes for a delightful, refreshing treat. ⏱⏱⏱

1 cup steamed and shredded chicken
$^1\!/_2$ medium head cabbage, finely cut
$^1\!/_4$ cup fish sauce
2 tablespoons finely chopped mint leaves
2 tablespoons finely chopped *rau ram* (polygonum) leaves
1 tablespoon sugar
2 tablespoons lime juice
$^1\!/_2$ teaspoon cracked black pepper

Garnish:

2 tablespoons sliced and fried shallots
2 tablespoons coarsely ground peanuts
$^1\!/_4$ cup cilantro leaves

In a large mixing bowl, combine all the ingredients and toss gently. Season to taste. Arrange in serving bowl topped with shallots, peanuts and cilantro.

Helpful hint: As with most salads, the cabbage leaves should be rinsed and spun dry, before slicing. A salad spinner is an easy and effective way to remove the excess water.

NAM XAO NUOC TUONG

A simple way of preparing mushrooms, in a sweet, soy sauce gravy. ⏱⏱⏱

8 ounces straw mushrooms
2 cloves garlic, crushed
1 tablespoon vegetable oil
Pinch of pepper
Pinch of salt
1 teaspoon sugar
3 tablespoons soy sauce
Fresh cracked pepper
Cilantro leaves

Rinse the mushrooms, pat dry on absorbent paper towels. Sauté garlic in oil until lightly browned and fragrant, add mushrooms, stirring quickly, then season with pepper, salt, sugar and soy sauce. Sauté until some liquid begins to evaporate; then remove from heat. Spoon onto a serving dish and sprinkle with fresh cracked pepper and cilantro leaves.

Helpful hint: Any variety of large mushrooms will work well in this recipe, and different types can be mixed together for variety.

Opposite:
*Cabbage Salad
with Chicken (left)
and Braised
Mushrooms with
Soy Sauce (right).*

BUN BO GIO HEO

Beef and Pork Leg Soup

Soups are an important part of the Vietnamese diet, often featured as a hearty main course or served in combination with a series of other dishes. ☺☺☺

8 cups lightly salted water
1 pound beef brisket
12 ounces leg of pork, cubed
1 stalk lemongrass, bruised
1 tablespoon shrimp paste
Salt
Pepper
1 tablespoon annatto seeds
2 tablespoons vegetable oil
10 shallots, thinly sliced
1 stalk lemongrass, finely chopped
2 red chilies, finely sliced
1/4 cup finely cut *ngo gai* (saw-leaf herb) leaves
1 pound fine rice noodles
1/4 cup finely cut baby leeks or spring onions
1/2 cup sliced or shaved banana blossom
1/2 cup bean sprouts
1/4 cup finely cut mint leaves
Juice of 2 limes

In a large soup pot, bring salted water to a boil. Add beef, pork and bruised lemongrass. Reduce heat and simmer for 90 minutes (or until meat is tender). Remove lemongrass and discard. Remove beef, cut into cubes and set aside. To the stock, add shrimp paste, and salt and pepper to taste. Simmer until needed.

Sauté the annatto seeds in oil, until the oil turns a light reddish color, then strain and discard the seeds. Reheat the oil and sauté the shallots until fragrant. Add chopped lemongrass and 1 of the chilies. Continue to sauté for a few more minutes, then add mixture to the stock with most of the *ngo gai* leaves.

Blanch rice noodles for 10–15 seconds, then place them in a large bowl. Top with beef, pork, baby leeks and the remaining *ngo gai* leaves. Pour in the hot soup broth.

Serve with banana blossom, bean sprouts, mint leaves, the remaining chili and freshly squeezed lime juice.

Helpful hint: Soup can easily be served throughout the day, or frozen and stored for use at another time, so recipes often call for large amounts of ingredients to accommodate making a large batch of soup at one time.

BUN THANG

Hanoi Chicken Soup

This is one of the many warming winter soups that has been popularized in Hanoi, and is now commonplace throughout the country. ☉☉☉

1 medium chicken
$\frac{1}{2}$ cup dried shrimp
12 ounces pork spareribs, cut into large pieces
12 cups lightly salted water
Pepper
Sugar
$\frac{1}{4}$ cup fish sauce
$\frac{1}{2}$ cup diced shallots
4 baby leek stalks or spring onions, finely cut
1 medium onion, sliced
4 cups fine rice noodles, blanched
1 egg, beaten, fried and cut into strips
10 ounces Vietnamese sausage, cut into thin strips
2 baby leek or spring onion greens, chopped
3 tablespoons finely chopped cilantro leaf
$\frac{1}{4}$ cup fried shallots
Fresh ground pepper
1 lime, cut into wedges
2 small red chilies, sliced
1 cup bean sprouts
1 medium head butter lettuce
1 cup shaved banana blossom
2 tablespoons shrimp paste

Boil chicken, dried shrimp and pork ribs in lightly salted water for about 20 minutes. Skim fat and season with pepper, sugar and fish sauce. Simmer for another 45 minutes, until the chicken is cooked. Remove both the chicken and shrimp. Let cool, then shred the chicken. Set aside. Add shallots, baby leeks and onion to the stock. Simmer for 20 minutes, season to taste.

Place a handful of the blanched rice noodles in a soup bowl and cover with a portion of the egg, chicken, spareribs, sausage, baby leek greens, cilantro and some of the fried shallots; add boiling stock to cover.

Sprinkle with freshly ground pepper, the remaining fried shallots and lime juice. Serve with chilies, bean sprouts, lettuce, banana blossom and shrimp paste.

Helpful hints: Vietnamese soups can be assembled in individual bowls or, as is often the case, set in one large bowl from which everyone helps themselves. In Vietnam, pork ribs are often steamed before cooking, for health purposes (which may not be necessary in many places) and to tenderize the meat.

PHO BO

Beef Noodle Soup

You'll find this soup everywhere in Vietnam—from street stalls to fancy restaurants. It is the classic breakfast meal, but it is just as delicious served any time of day or night. ⏱⏱⏱

1 medium piece of fresh ginger root
1 large onion
12 cups water
2 pounds beef bones
12 ounces beef brisket
Pinch of salt
3 pieces star anise
1 cinnamon stick
Salt
Pepper
1 cup bean sprouts
8 ounces flat rice noodles
8 ounces raw beef sirloin, thinly sliced
1 medium onion, sliced
$\frac{1}{4}$ cup finely cut baby leeks or spring onions
$\frac{1}{2}$ cup chopped *ngo gai* (saw-leaf herb) leaves
$\frac{1}{2}$ cup chopped cilantro leaves

Garnish:

1 tablespoon chili sauce
3 tablespoons Yellow Bean Sauce (see page 37)
2 small red chilies, sliced
2 limes, cut into wedges
Mint leaves
Ngo gai leaves
Cilantro leaves

Grill ginger and onion until the skins are burnt. In a deep pan, combine water, bones and beef brisket. Bring to a boil, skimming frequently, to remove residue. Add salt, grilled ginger and onion, star anise and cinnamon. After 45 minutes, remove the tender cooked beef and slice it very finely. Strain the soup into a separate container, adding salt and pepper to taste.

Wash and drain bean sprouts. Quickly blanch rice noodles and bean sprouts in boiling water, to soften, but do not overcook. Arrange in a soup bowl. Top with sliced beef brisket, raw beef sirloin, sliced onion, chopped baby leeks, *ngo gai* and cilantro leaves. Pour the boiling soup into the bowl and sprinkle with freshly ground pepper. By that time the raw beef should be medium-cooked.

Serve with chili and Yellow Bean Sauces, sliced chilies, lime wedges, mint, *ngo gai* and cilantro leaves.

Helpful hints: Grilling the ginger and onion can be done either over an open flame or simply in a pan. Chicken is a delicious alternative to beef, and most Vietnamese restaurants offer both versions.

BUN RIEU

Crab Soup

The dark brown crab found in rice fields—pulled out of the mud with a stick—is used to make this savory dish. All parts of the paddy field crab are used, including the residue strained from the soup during the slow cooking process, which becomes a kind of fish cake or mousse that can be added to the soup. ⏱⏱⏱

2 pounds paddy field or mud crab
Salt
Water
1 large tomato, cut in 6 pieces and seeded
3 cloves garlic, crushed
2 tablespoons chopped baby leeks
2 tablespoons fish sauce
1 tablespoon tamarind pulp
8 ounces fried bean curd
Sugar
Salt
1 tablespoon shrimp paste
1 pound rice noodles

Garnish:
$\frac{1}{4}$ cup cilantro leaves
$\frac{1}{4}$ cup shredded banana blossom
1 red chili, finely sliced
$\frac{1}{2}$ cup bean sprouts
$\frac{1}{4}$ cup mint leaves
$\frac{1}{2}$ cup shredded water spinach
$\frac{1}{4}$ cup *ngo gai* leaves (saw-leaf herb)
1 lime, cut in wedges

Rinse crabs. Remove the top shell and rinse again, then drain. Place crabs in a large bowl and pound with some salt, add water, stir and strain to obtain crab liquid (use a sieve). Pound crab sediments again and set aside.

In a large soup pot, bring crab liquid to a boil. When crab meat floats on the surface, reduce heat to simmer. Clarify liquid and set residue aside (this should form a dense crab patty).

In a separate pan, stir-fry the tomatoes with the garlic, baby leeks and fish sauce, then add tamarind pulp and bean curd. Season with sugar, salt and shrimp paste, then add to crab. Simmer for a few minutes. To serve, place rice noodles in a bowl, pour in the soup.

Serve with cilantro leaves, banana blossom, chili, bean sprouts, mint leaves, water spinach, *ngo gai* and a few wedges of lime.

Helpful hints: The standard garnish of leaves is also served with the various hand rolls. Since paddy field crab is difficult to find, try using whatever small variety of crab is available.

CANH BAP CAI CUON THIT & DUA DAU HEO

Cabbage Roll Soup & Preserved Pork Head Meat

CANH BAP CAI CUON THIT

This classic soup is very popular during Tet, the Vietnamese New Year celebration. ⏱⏱

1 cup ground pork
$^{1}/_{2}$ cup minced shrimp
5 shallots, finely chopped
Salt
Freshly ground pepper
1 pound white cabbage leaves, blanched
20 whole baby leek or spring onion greens, blanched
6 cups chicken or pork stock
2 tablespoons diced baby leek or spring onion stalks
1 tablespoon cilantro, finely chopped
2 tablespoons fish sauce

In a large bowl, mix pork, shrimp and shallots. Season with salt and pepper. Put a tablespoon of the mixture into each cabbage leaf, roll and use the baby leek greens to tie the rolls into parcels.

Cook the parcels in salted water for 5 minutes and serve with the chicken or pork stock. Sprinkle with baby leeks, cilantro and freshly ground pepper. Serve with fish sauce, as a dip.

Helpful hint: The cabbage should be blanched first in boiling water (not in the stock) to remove the bitterness and to soften it for rolling.

DUA DAU HEO ⏱⏱⏱

1 pound pig's head meat
1 cup water
2 teaspoons baking soda
2 cups white vinegar
2 tablespoons sugar
1 tablespoon salt
2 cloves garlic, crushed
1 medium red chili, seeded and sliced
1 teaspoon whole black peppercorns
1 tablespoon peeled and sliced ginger root
1 clove garlic, finely sliced
$^{1}/_{4}$ cup cilantro leaves
1 chili flower for garnish

Clean pork in water with baking soda and boil in lightly salted water until thoroughly cooked. When cool, cut into $1^{1}/_{4}$-inch pieces and rinse with cold water. Combine vinegar, sugar and salt, bring to a boil, then remove from heat and allow to cool.

Place pork in a jar, add crushed garlic, chili, peppercorns and ginger. Cover with liquid and seal the jar. Let set for a few hours.

When the pork is white and crunchy (you should taste to determine when the texture is right), and a little bit sweet and sour, it is ready to eat. Finely slice the meat, add garlic and toss well in a bowl. Garnish with cilantro leaves and red chili shreds.

CANH NGHIEU

Clam Soup

This unusual recipe is quite easy to prepare, and like many of the soups in Vietnam, relies heavily on fresh ingredients. Starfruit, also known as carambola, is increasingly available in specialty food shops. Thin slices of fresh, tart pineapple can also be used. ① ① ①

    24 clams, washed and cleaned
    6 cups chicken stock
    2 tablespoons finely chopped baby leeks or
        spring onions
    2 cloves garlic, finely chopped
    1 tablespoon vegetable oil
    2 tablespoons fish sauce
    1 teaspoon shrimp paste (optional)
    2 medium starfruit, sliced

Garnish:
    ½ cup cilantro leaves
    2 red chilies, seeded and finely sliced
    ½ cup *rau ram* (polygonum) leaves

Rinse clams thoroughly. Bring stock to a boil, add clams and cook, stirring until the shells open. Remove the clam meat, discarding the shells, and set aside. In a separate pan, fry the baby leek and garlic in oil until soft, add clams and season with fish sauce and shrimp paste. Return stock to a boil. Add clam mixture and starfruit, and immediately turn off the heat. Garnish with cilantro, chili and *rau ram*.

Helpful hints: This is an ideal recipe for mussels. If available, use the small, green-lipped variety. For many of the fish soups, chicken or pork stock are commonly used. If you prefer, a clear vegetable or fish stock may also be used.

CANH CHUA CA LOC

Tamarind Snake-headed Mullet Soup

This recipe calls for the firm white-fleshed snake-headed mullet, also called mud-fish, which has a strong "fishy" flavor. The use of tamarind is similar to a Thai *tom yam*, but this soup is not as spicy. The addition of tomato, pineapple and fresh herbs imparts a fragrant flavor. ☺☺☺

1 pound snake-headed mullet
4 cups fish stock
1/4 pineapple, peeled and sliced
1/4 cup sliced mint leaves
1 small red chili, seeded and sliced
2 pieces okra (lady's fingers), sliced
1/2 cup sliced taro stem
1/4 cup tamarind pulp
1/4 cup bean sprouts
1 tomato, cut into wedges
Salt
Pepper
3 tablespoons fish sauce
1 tablespoon sugar
2 tablespoons fried shallots
2 tablespoons chopped cilantro leaves
1 tablespoon chopped *rau ram* (polygonum) leaves
1 tablespoon chopped *ngo gai* (saw-leaf herb) leaves
Freshly ground pepper

Blanch fish for about 5 minutes in boiling stock, then remove from the heat and strain, keeping both the stock and the fish.

In a large pan, bring stock to boil again. Add the pineapple, mint, chili, okra and taro. Reduce heat and simmer for 3–4 minutes, then add the tamarind pulp, bean sprouts and tomato. Bring to a boil again. Skim the top and season with salt, pepper, fish sauce and sugar. Place a portion of the fish in a soup bowl, spoon in a ladle of stock and garnish with fried shallots, cilantro, *rau ram* and *ngo gai* leaves. Finish with freshly ground pepper.

Helpful hints: The leaves are used here to help mellow the flavor of the snake-headed mullet. Any firm-textured fish is a good substitute.

CA TIM NUONG

Grilled Eggplant with Crab

This recipe is common to Cambodia and southern Vietnam and makes surprising use of eggplant, one of the many vegetables grown in central Vietnam. 🕐🕐

6 long (Japanese) eggplants
¼ cup cooking oil
3 tablespoons chopped shallots
1½ cups fresh crabmeat
3 tablespoons sliced baby leeks or spring onions
3 tablespoons crushed peanuts
¼ cup fish sauce
Cilantro leaves

Cut eggplants in half and brush with some of the oil. Grill over an open flame or under a broiler, turning regularly, until the skin turns a darkish brown and the flesh is soft. Peel off the skin and discard. Fry the shallots in the remaining oil. Place eggplant on a serving plate and sprinkle with crabmeat, baby leeks, peanuts and shallots. Toss with fish sauce. Garnish with a few sprigs of cilantro.

Helpful hint: Preparing crabmeat is very time consuming. Save a few steps and buy fresh, prepared crabmeat from your local fish market.

DAU HU CHIEN SA & RAU XAO

Fried Bean Curd with Lemongrass & Stir-Fried Vegetables with Fish Sauce

DAU HU CHIEN SA

These vegetable dishes cater to the strict and not-so-strict vegetarian. ☻☻

1 cup peanut oil
1¼ pounds bean curd, cut into 1-inch x 2-inch pieces
3 tablespoons finely chopped lemongrass
1 red chili, finely chopped
2 cloves garlic, chopped
1 tablespoon vegetable oil
1 teaspoon five-spice powder
Salt
Pepper

Opposite: Fried Bean Curd with Lemongrass (left) and Stir-Fried Vegetables with Fish Sauce (right).

Heat peanut oil in deep pan, fry bean curd in hot oil, drain on absorbent paper towels, set aside. In a separate sauté pan or wok, sauté the lemongrass, chili and garlic in hot vegetable oil until soft. Add the bean curd and mix well. Season with five-spice powder, salt and pepper. Set on a serving platter.

Helpful hint: Fried bean curd is available in Asian grocery stores, which makes preparing this dish a snap.

RAU XAO ☻☻☻

12 cups salted water
1 cup sliced carrots
1 cup cauliflower pieces
1 cup baby corn
1 cup black mushrooms
1 cup tender kale or broccoli stems
2 tablespoons vegetable oil
1 tablespoon rice wine
2 tablespoons fish sauce
2 cloves garlic, crushed
Salt
Pepper

Blanch the vegetables in lightly salted boiling water, remove and place in a large bowl of cold water. Using a wok or large sauté pan, heat the oil, then stir-fry the drained vegetables, adding the rice wine. Finish the stir-fry with fish sauce and garlic. Season with salt and pepper to taste. Serve with steamed rice.

Helpful hint: When blanching vegetables, they should remain in the water just long enough to slightly soften. Place them in cold (or iced) water immediately after cooking to ensure a crisp texture.

CANH BI RO HAM DUA & RAU MUONG XAO TUONG

Braised Pumpkin with Coconut Milk & Pan-Fried Water Spinach with Yellow Bean Sauce

CANH BI RO HAM DUA

This is a traditional Buddhist vegetarian dish finished with raw peanuts. ⊘⊘⊘

- **2 cups peeled and cubed pumpkin ($^3/_4$ -inch cubes)**
- **2 cups thin coconut milk**
- **2 cups cubed sweet potato or taro root ($^3/_4$-inch cubes)**
- **$^1/_2$ cup wood ear mushrooms**
- **$^1/_4$ cup thick coconut cream**
- **$^1/_2$ cup raw peanuts, soaked in warm water**
- **$^1/_2$ cup thinly sliced loofah (or green zucchini)**
- **Salt**
- **1 teaspoon sugar**
- **Cilantro leaves**
- **2 tablespoon sliced *rau ram* (polygonum) leaves**

Place pumpkin and thin coconut milk in a deep sauté pan. Bring to a boil. Cook until pumpkin is half-done. Add the sweet potatoes and wood ear mushrooms to the pumpkin mixture. Reduce heat and simmer until nearly done. Add thick coconut cream, peanuts, loofah and bring to a boil again. Remove from heat. Season to taste with salt and sugar.

Serve in a bowl and sprinkle with fresh cilantro and *rau ram* leaves.

RAU MUONG XAO TUONG

Water spinach, which is available in many specialist Asian grocery shops, has hollow, straw-like stems that are crunchy when eaten. The best substitute is mature spinach. ⊘⊘

- **1 pound water spinach, washed**
- **2 cloves garlic, crushed**
- **2 baby leeks or spring onions, finely sliced (white part only)**
- **2 tablespoons vegetable oil**
- **2 tablespoons Yellow Bean Sauce (see page 37)**
- **Salt**
- **Pepper**

Blanch spinach in boiling water and drain well. Fry garlic and leeks in oil until soft, then add spinach and Yellow Bean Sauce. Fry over high heat. Season with salt and pepper.

Helpful hint: This is another dish suited to the wok that requires only a few minutes to cook.

COM NGHIEU & COM HOANG BAO

Clam Rice & Imperial Rice

COM NGHIEU ⌚⌚⌚

2 pounds clams, washed well in cold water
½ cup water
2 tablespoons lard (or oil)
2 tablespoons pork cracklings
½ cup finely shaved banana blossom
1 starfruit, thinly sliced
2 tablespoons sesame seeds, roasted
5 cups cooked white rice
2 tablespoons finely chopped *rau ram* (polygonum)
1 cup sesame seed rice crackers, baked and broken into small pieces
2 tablespoons chili sauce
1 teaspoon shrimp paste
1 tablespoon vinegar
1 teaspoon lime juice
Pinch of sugar

Opposite: *Clam Rice (left) and Imperial Rice (right) with chili sauce.*

Steam the clams until they open. Drain, remove meat and set aside. Discard shells. Strain the stock and reduce by one-third, then remove from heat.

Heat pork fat and sauté pork cracklings, add banana blossom, starfruit and sesame seeds. Cook gently for 3 minutes or until sesame seeds are lightly browned. Add rice and clam stock. Stir-fry for 3 minutes. Before removing from heat, add clams, *rau ram*, rice crackers, and season to taste.

Serve with chili sauce, and shrimp paste mixed with vinegar, lime juice and sugar.

COM HOANG BAO

Vietnamese are fond of adding pork (or pork fat) for extra flavor to nearly anything that might appear to be an all fish or vegetarian dish. Often it is essential. Other times it might not be a necessary ingredient. It's always a good idea to experiment. ⌚⌚⌚

4 shallots, chopped
2 tablespoons cooking oil
4 ounces pork (or chicken), diced (1 cup)
4 ounces small shrimp (1 cup)
4 ounces dried lotus seeds, boiled and drained
¼ teaspoon salt
1 pinch pepper
1 bowl steamed rice
1 egg, fried and chopped (optional)
1 large lotus leaf
2 baby leeks or spring onions, chopped

Quickly sauté shallots in oil. Add pork, shrimp, lotus seeds, salt and pepper. Cook until done. Mix with steamed rice and stir well. If egg is used, add to the fried mixture at the same time as the rice. Remove from heat and place on lotus leaf. Sprinkle with chopped baby leek. Fold into a neat package.

Helpful hint: As a substitute for lotus leaf, use a large grape or fig leaf.

MAM KHO

Preserved Salted Fish Stew

This is a hearty soup recipe that calls for *mam sac* (salted fish), considered a delicacy in Vietnam. ①①①

2 tablespoons vegetable oil
3 cloves garlic, finely chopped
$\frac{1}{2}$ cup finely chopped shallots
$\frac{1}{4}$ cup sliced fresh pork belly or pancetta
$\frac{1}{3}$ cup finely chopped lemongrass
$\frac{1}{2}$ cup shrimp, peeled and washed
$\frac{1}{2}$ teaspoon cracked black pepper
1 cup water
10 ounces salted fish (*mam sac*)
10 ounces snake-head mullet
2 small red chilies, seeded and sliced
$1\frac{1}{2}$ cups cubed eggplant (1 medium)
2 teaspoons sugar

Garnish:
2 cups fragrant leaves
2 cups shaved water spinach stems
2 limes, cut into wedges
2 cups bean sprouts
2 cups sliced cucumber
1 head lettuce
1 cup banana blossom
2 cups peeled and sliced lotus stems

Heat oil in a large pan, add garlic, shallots, pork belly and lemongrass. Sauté until soft. Add shrimp, toss quickly until heated through, season with pepper.

In a large saucepan, add water and both types of fish; bring to a boil. Simmer for 15 minutes or until the fish completely breaks apart. Remove fish and set aside. Remove bones and discard. Strain the stock, then boil again with 2 pieces of chili, all of the shrimp/pork mixture, eggplant and sugar. Simmer for 10 minutes or until reduced by one-third. Set a portion of the fish in individual bowls. Add stock.

Serve with fragrant leaves, sliced water spinach stems, lime wedges, bean sprouts, cucumber, lettuce, banana blossom and lotus root.

Helpful hints: There are many different grades of *mam sac*, however, any dried or salted fish will work with this recipe—cod is a good choice. Soak the salted fish in water for 10–15 minutes and brush clean to remove any dirt or impurities. For the fresh fish, use a whole fish, or just the head, which is considered a delicacy. Any firm-fleshed fish can replace the snake-headed mullet.

MUC NHOI THIT

Stuffed Squid

Another interesting recipe featuring squid, this time using the whole body. ☺☺☺

10 medium washed and cleaned squid. (Use the tentacles in the stuffing mixture and save the sacs for stuffing)

Stuffing:

1 tablespoon peanut oil
3 tablespoons finely sliced shallots
1 clove garlic, finely sliced
1 pound lean leanground pork
$1/4$ cup cellophane noodles
6 wood ear mushrooms, finely chopped
1 teaspoon five-spice powder
1 tablespoon soy sauce
10 sets of squid tentacles, finely chopped

Seasoning:

Pinch salt
Pinch pepper
1 teaspoon sugar

Sauce and Garnish:

$1/4$ cup diced shallots
3 cloves garlic, crushed
$1/4$ cup butter or oil

3 large tomatoes, peeled, seeded and chopped
Salt and pepper
Cilantro leaves
Fresh ground pepper

For the **stuffing**, heat oil in pan, add shallots and garlic, cook, stirring until soft. Combine shallot mixture with the other stuffing ingredients in a bowl and mix well. Add **seasoning**. Stuff the squid sacs with the mixture and secure with a small toothpick.

To prepare the **sauce**, sauté shallots and garlic in butter until soft. Add stuffed squid and sauté on both sides for about 10 minutes or until slightly browned and cooked through. Remove from pan, set aside and keep warm. Add tomatoes, salt and pepper to taste to the pan, and simmer until the tomatoes have been reduced to a thick sauce. Place squid on a large platter and remove toothpicks. Pour the tomato sauce over the squid. Garnish with cilantro and fresh ground pepper.

Helpful hints: When serving, you can leave the squid whole or cut into more manageable pieces. For a variation on the cooking technique, try grilling the squid.

MUC NUONG

Grilled Squid

Grilled meats and seafood are very popular in Vietnam and many recipes, like this one, rely upon the specific flavors imparted from the open wood burning grill. ◔◔◔

1 pound cleaned squid
1 tablespoon salt
½ cup cilantro leaves

Marinade:
Pinch of pepper
2 cloves garlic, crushed
2 tablespoons peanut oil
1 teaspoon five-spice powder
1 teaspoon curry powder
1 tablespoon finely chopped lemongrass
1 tablespoon thick soy sauce
1 teaspoon sesame oil
1 tablespoon lime juice
1 teaspoon sugar

Rub the squid with salt and rinse. Slit and flatten the squid sac and make diagonal cuts on the inside surface. Cut into bite-sized pieces. Combine marinade ingredients, then marinate squid for 1 hour.

Grill squid over a charcoal grill, until just tender (about 2 minutes each side). Arrange on a serving platter and garnish with cilantro. Serve with Fish Sauce Dip (see page 37).

Helpful hint: This is a versatile marinade, suitable for other types of fish or poultry.

TOM CANG KHO & MUC XAO THAP CAM

Spicy River Prawns & Fried Squid with Vegetables

TOM CANG KHO

This is a southern recipe that calls for giant, fresh-water prawns, which are often as big as lobsters. Crayfish or baby lobsters can also be used. ◑◐

3 cloves garlic, finely diced
1 small red chili, finely chopped
2 tablespoons cooking oil
1 teaspoon cracked black peppercorns
2 tablespoons sugar
$^1/_4$ cup fish sauce
$^1/_2$ cup water
6 giant prawns, unpeeled
$^1/_2$ cup cilantro leaves

Opposite: Spicy River Prawns (left) and Fried Squid with Vegetables (right).

In a deep pan, sauté garlic and chili in oil until soft. Add peppercorns, sugar, fish sauce, water and prawns. Cook uncovered for 10 minutes, or until the prawns turn bright pink. Remove prawns and arrange on a platter. Reduce the stock until slightly sticky. Pour over the prawns and garnish with cilantro.

Helpful hint: Since this recipe uses giant prawns which could be difficult to find, you may have to increase the number of smaller shrimp, or try using lobster or crayfish.

MUC XAO THAP CAM ◑◑◐

3 cloves garlic, finely diced
$^1/_4$ cup vegetable oil
$1^1/_2$ pounds cleaned squid, cut with diagonal slits
2 medium carrots, sliced
$^1/_2$ cup chopped celery
1 medium onion, cut into small segments
1 teaspoon salt
2 teaspoon cracked black peppercorns
1 cup snow peas
2 tomatoes, cut into wedges
$^1/_4$ large pineapple, thinly sliced
3 tablespoons fish sauce
Fresh ground pepper
Cilantro leaves

Sauté half of the garlic in 2 tablespoons of oil until fragrant, then add squid. Cook for about 2 minutes, or until just tender. Set aside.

In a separate pan, sauté remaining garlic in oil until fragrant. Add carrot, celery, onion, salt and pepper, and sauté for 3 minutes or until tender. Add snow peas, tomatoes, pineapple and fish sauce, then the squid. Continue to cook until squid is heated through, about 1 minute. Serve on a large platter. Season with freshly ground pepper and garnish with cilantro.

Serve with steamed rice, soy sauce, Fish Sauce Dip (see page 37) and chilies.

CUA RANG VOI SOT ME

Crab with Tamarind Sauce

This is what they're eating at those crowded tables on the sidewalks of Ho Chi Minh City—a taste sensation. ☺☺☺

> 4 whole medium crabs
> Peanut oil for deep-frying
> 1 tablespoon tamarind pulp
> $\frac{1}{4}$ cup rice wine
> 4 cloves garlic, chopped
> 2 tablespoons vegetable oil
> $\frac{1}{4}$ cup chopped baby leeks or spring onions
>   (white part only), cut in 1-inch pieces
> 3 tablespoons fish sauce
> 1 teaspoon crushed white pepper

Clean the crabs, take off the tops, rinse thoroughly, cut in half and break the claws. Heat peanut oil in wok until very hot, deep-fry crabs for 30 seconds, or until color changes. Set on paper towels to absorb excess oil.

Dissolve tamarind pulp in rice wine. In a large pan or wok, sauté garlic in vegetable oil until soft, add crab and continue cooking for 2–3 minutes on a high heat. Add tamarind mixture, fish sauce and pepper. Reduce for another 2 minutes, then add baby leeks. Remove from heat. Place crabs on a platter and pour tamarind sauce over. Serve with steamed rice.

Helpful hints: Although this dish is traditionally prepared in a wok, the use of a deep-fryer might make the cooking easier. You can also substitute freshly ground black pepper, although white pepper is often the preferred ingredient of Vietnamese cooks.

CUA HAP BIA

Crab in Beer Broth

Beer is a popular drink in Vietnam, but it also makes for a delicious broth. This is an innovative dish said to have been developed by an early French colonial administrator. ☺☺☺

6 whole large crabs, rinsed and cleaned

Marinade:
Salt
Pepper
1 teaspoon sesame oil
1 tablespoon oyster sauce
3 cloves garlic, finely sliced

Marinate the crab with salt, pepper, sesame oil, oyster sauce and a clove of garlic for 1 hour.

1 large onion, sliced
2 tablespoons vegetable oil
2 small red chilies, sliced
6 ounces beer
2 medium tomatoes, diced
1 tablespoon fried garlic or shallots
1 cup watercress

Sauté remaining garlic and onion in oil for 2–3 minutes, or until brown. Add crab and chilies, and continue frying. After a few minutes, add beer and cover. Reduce heat, and cook for 10 minutes. Add tomatoes. Cover again. Cook for 5 more minutes.

Serve in bowls, adding a little of the broth. Garnish with fried garlic and watercress.

Helpful hint: Almost any variety of hard-shell crab can be used for this recipe.

CUA VA NGHIEU LAN BOT CHIEN GION

Crispy Soft-Shell Crabs and Clams

This is a dish that can be served as a main course or an appetizer. It's similar to English fish and chips but with an Asian twist. ⊘⊘⊘

    12 clams, soaked in water for 1 hour
    8 cups lightly salted water
    6 soft-shell crabs, cleaned and trimmed
    Oil for deep-frying
    Cilantro (for garnish)

Marinade:

    1 teaspoon sesame oil
    1 tablespoon garlic oil
    2 teaspoons pepper
    1 teaspoon salt

Boil clams in salted water until they open. Remove meat. For the **marinade**, combine ingredients, add crab and clams, and leave for 45 minutes.

Batter:

    1 cup all-purpose flour
    1 cup rice flour
    Water
    1 tablespoon vinegar
    2 tablespoons soy sauce
    1 teaspoon annatto seed oil (see page 64)
    1 teaspoon sugar

To prepare the **batter**, turn the crabs and clams in the combined flours, making sure both sides are well dusted. Combine all the batter ingredients (including the remaining flour) in a large bowl. Dip the clams and crabs into the batter, ensuring they are evenly coated. Deep-fry the battered crabs and clams until golden brown. Remove and set on absorbent paper towels to soak up any excess oil.

Garnish with cilantro. Serve with chili, soy sauce and Sweet and Sour Sauce (page 38).

Helpful hint: Rather than deep-frying, this is a good recipe for pan-frying (Western-style) in butter. Use a large pan or skillet, and a very hot flame, making sure not to burn the butter. Cook for 2–3 minutes on each side.

CA MU CHIEN VOI GUNG & CA CHEP KHO RIENG

Fried Grouper with Ginger Sauce & Braised Carp with Galangal Sauce

CA MU CHIEN VOI GUNG

Vietnam boasts an abundance of ocean and fresh-water fish. Ginger and galangal, both members of the ginger family, have been used to impart their unique flavors to these fish dishes. ⊘ ⊘

1 tablespoon salt
1 tablespoon pepper
1 grouper fish, $1\frac{1}{2}$–$1\frac{3}{4}$ pounds, slit on both sides
3 tablespoons oil
2 tablespoons chopped green baby leeks or spring onions

Sauce:
3 tablespoons finely sliced ginger root
3 tablespoons finely sliced lemongrass
2 red chilies, finely sliced
2 black mushrooms, finely sliced
2 tablespoons soy sauce
1 cup fish sauce

Combine the **sauce** ingredients: ginger, lemongrass, chilies, mushrooms, soy sauce and fish sauce. Set aside for 2 hours.

Opposite: Fried Grouper with Ginger Sauce (left) and Braised Carp with Galangal Sauce (right).

Salt and pepper the fish and let rest for 1 hour, then brush with oil and grill slowly on both sides until fish is cooked. Place on a large platter, pour the sauce over the fish and garnish with baby leeks.

CA CHEP KHO RIENG ⊘ ⊘

6 carp, cut into 4-ounce steaks
3 tablespoons vegetable oil
2 tablespoons finely sliced galangal
4 tablespoons fish sauce
4 tablespoons Caramel Syrup (see page 38)
Salt
Pepper

Sauté carp in oil with galangal. Add fish sauce and caramel syrup, braise slowly on both sides until fish is done. Season with salt and pepper. Arrange on a platter. Serve with steamed rice.

Helpful hint: Both of these recipes can be used with a variety of whole fish, steaks or fillets.

LUON XAO LAN XUC BANH TRANG ME & CA NAU NGOT

Minced Eel with Sesame Seed Rice Crackers & River Fish with Dill and Tomato

LUON XAO LAN XUC BANH TRANG ME

This recipe must have been created to make use of those delightful sesame rice crackers—the mixture is perfect for dipping into. ⏀⏀⏀

- 1 tablespoon diced garlic
- 2 tablespoons diced shallots
- 2 tablespoons finely chopped lemongrass
- 1 tablespoon finely chopped red chili
- 3 tablespoons finely chopped wood ear mushrooms
- 2 tablespoons vegetable oil
- 1 tablespoon five-spice powder
- 1 tablespoon Vietnamese curry powder
- $3/4$ pound baby eel, finely chopped
- 2 tablespoons coarsely chopped peanuts
- $1/2$ cup cilantro leaves
- 1 red chili, thinly sliced
- Sesame seed rice crackers

Sauté garlic, shallots, lemongrass, chili and mushrooms in the oil. Add five-spice powder, curry and eel. Sauté for 5 minutes, or until eel is cooked. Place on a platter and garnish with peanuts, cilantro and chili. Serve with crackers.

Helpful hint: Wood ear mushrooms are used, primarily for texture. However, any fresh mushroom that adds texture and flavor is a good substitute. Some dried varieties will also work.

CA NAU NGOT ⏀⏀

- 6 cups light chicken stock
- $1^1/4$ pounds freshwater fish fillets, cut into large chunks
- 2 medium tomatoes, cut into wedges
- Salt
- Pepper
- 1 tablespoon chopped dill
- Fresh dill

Bring stock to a boil, add fish and simmer for 5 minutes. Skim the top, add the tomatoes and season with salt, pepper and dill. Cook another few minutes. Garnish with fresh dill before serving.

GOI VIT BAP CHUOI & VIT KHO GUNG

Banana Blossom Salad with Duck and Ginger & Braised Duck with Ginger

GOI VIT BAP CHUOI ☺☺☺

1 young banana blossom, finely cut
2 cups iced water
1 tablespoon lemon juice
2 duck breasts
$1/2$ cup Fish Sauce Dip (see page 37)
1 teaspoon finely cut *rau ram* (polygonum
   leaves)
1 tablespoon finely chopped ginger root
1 tablespoon coarsely ground peanuts
1 tablespoon fried shallots
$1/4$ cup cilantro leaves

Opposite: Banana Blossom Salad with Duck and Ginger (left) and Braised Duck with Ginger (right).

Place the sliced banana blossom in cold water with lemon juice, and let soak for 1 hour. Boil (or steam) the duck in a shallow saucepan with a little water until tender. Let cool, remove skin and cut into thin slices. Drain the banana blossom, then toss in a large bowl with Fish Sauce Dip, *rau ram*, ginger, peanuts and the sliced duck. Arrange on a platter and sprinkle with fried shallots. Garnish with cilantro leaves.

Helpful hints: If you can't find banana blossom, use shaved celery. In addition to boiling, the duck breast can be baked, fried or grilled.

VIT KHO GUNG ☺☺☺

1 whole duck
$1/4$ cup finely sliced ginger root
1 tablespoon salt
3 tablespoons vegetable oil
4 tablespoons fish sauce
1 tablespoon sugar
2 cups boiling water
1 red chili, sliced
1 teaspoon pepper
$1/4$ cup cilantro leaves

Rub the duck with half the ginger and salt, then rinse and cut into 8 pieces. Heat oil and fry duck slowly until the skin looks nice and brown, then add remaining ginger, fish sauce and sugar. Keep frying, then cover with boiling water, add chili and pepper, and simmer until duck is tender. Remove from heat. Garnish with cilantro leaves.

GA QUAY MAT ONG

Honey-Roasted Chicken

This recipe works well with any type of fowl or game. Since considerable time is involved with the marinades and cooking, it is probably best suited for a large bird and special occasion. ⏰ ⏰ ⏰

1 large, whole chicken

Marinade I:
1 teaspoon pepper
1 teaspoon salt
1 tablespoon sugar
1 teaspoon sesame oil

Marinade II:
3 tablespoons honey
2 tablespoons sweet soy sauce
1 tablespoon lime juice
1 tablespoon annatto seed oil (see page 64)
1 teaspoon sesame oil

Marinade III:
1 teaspoon pepper
1 teaspoon salt
1 tablespoon sugar
1 teaspoon sesame oil

Combine all the **marinade I** ingredients. Rub into the inside of the chicken and close with a needle or a bamboo stick. Marinate for 1 hour.

Set chicken in a baking pan. Combine **marinade II** ingredients. Pour over chicken. Place in oven at 375°F.

Mix the **marinade III** ingredients. Baste the chicken with this marinade every 10–15 minutes. Bake until skin is a golden brown and chicken is well cooked.

Cut up the chicken and assemble on a serving platter. Serve with deep-fried sweet buns or steamed sticky rice.

Helpful hint: Basting is the secret to this recipe.

CA RI GA NUOC COT DUA

Chicken Curry in Coconut Milk

Curried dishes have traditionally been associated with Buddhists, and there are a number of popular recipes where curry is the featured spice. This is one of the best. ☺☺☺

> 1 whole chicken, deboned, skinned and cut into large cubes
> 3 cloves garlic, finely chopped
> 3 tablespoons curry powder
> 1 onion, cut in thick slices
> 1 red chili, sliced
> 1 stalk lemongrass, bruised
> 3 tablespoons annatto seed oil (see page 64)
> 1 teaspoon salt
> 1 tablespoon pepper
> 1 tablespoon sugar
> $1/3$ cup coconut milk
> 1 cup peeled and cubed sweet potatoes (taro root or potato can be substituted), blanched

Marinade:

> 2 tablespoons garlic oil
> 1 red chili, finely chopped
> $1/3$ stalk lemongrass, finely chopped
> 1 small piece ginger root, finely chopped
> 2 tablespoons curry powder

Combine ingredients for **marinade**, pour over chicken and let stand for 1 hour.

Sauté garlic, curry powder, onion, chili and lemongrass stalk in the annatto seed oil for 2 minutes. Add chicken, salt, pepper and sugar, and continue frying for another few minutes. Then add coconut milk, reduce heat and simmer slowly. Add sweet potato. Cook for 10 minutes or until both the chicken and sweet potato are done. Remove from heat and discard lemongrass. Serve in individual bowls.

Helpful hint: French bread or a baguette is recommended to serve with this curry, along with chilies and the Salt, Pepper and Lime Mix (see page 39).

GA XAO HOT DIEU & VIT NAU CAM

Stir-Fried Chicken with Mango and Cashews & Spicy Duck in Orange Sauce

GA XAO HOT DIEU

Quick deep-frying of the chicken at the beginning of this recipe produces exquisitely tender pieces of chicken. ☺☺☺

4 boneless, skinless chicken breasts, cut into cubes
Oil for deep-frying
3 tablespoons vegetable oil
1 tablespoon chopped garlic
1 red chili, sliced
1/2 cup snow peas, blanched
3 tablespoons fish sauce
1 teaspoon lime juice
Sugar
Salt
Pepper
1/2 cup chopped mango
1/2 cup chopped tomato
1/2 cup cashew nuts

Opposite: Stir-Fried Chicken with Mango and Cashews (left) and Spicy Duck in Orange Sauce (right).

Deep-fry chicken in hot oil for 4–5 minutes or until nearly cooked. Remove from fryer. In a separate pan, heat the vegetable oil and sauté the garlic and red chili for 1 minute. Add the chicken and continue cooking for another minute. Add snow peas, fish sauce, lime juice, sugar, salt and pepper to taste. Just before serving, add mango and tomato. Garnish with cashews.

VIT NAU CAM ☺☺☺

1 duck (approximately 4 pounds)
Oil for frying
1 small red chili, sliced
2 tablespoons sugar
2 cups orange juice
Orange segments
Candied orange peel

Marinade:

1 tablespoon finely chopped ginger
1 tablespoon finely chopped red chili
2 tablespoons fish sauce
Salt and pepper to taste

Combine ingredients for **marinade**. Let duck marinate for 1 hour.

Fry marinated duck in oil until golden brown. Add **marinade**, then reduce heat. Add sugar and continue cooking until sugar begins to caramelize slightly, then add orange juice. Braise another few minutes, then remove duck. Reduce sauce to desired consistency. Pour over duck just prior to serving. Garnish with orange segments, orange peel, and chili.

Helpful hint: You may prefer to roast the duck in the oven. If so, baste regularly.

DUI ECH XAO SA OT & OC NHOI THIT

Sautéed Frogs' Legs with Lemongrass & Snails Stuffed with Minced Pork

DUI ECH XAO SA OT ☺☺☺

8 double frogs' legs
Oil for deep-frying
3 tablespoons vegetable oil
1 stalk lemongrass, finely chopped
1 clove garlic, finely chopped
1 red chili, finely chopped
1 tablespoon mixed curry powder
2 tablespoons fish sauce
Salt
Pepper
Sugar
$^1/_4$ cup chicken stock (see page 39)

Opposite: Sautéed Frogs' Legs with Lemongrass (left) and Snails Stuffed with Minced Pork (right).

Deep-fry frogs' legs until nearly cooked. Remove from fryer. In a large pan (or wok) heat the vegetable oil. Add lemongrass, garlic, chili and frogs' legs, and sauté, adding curry powder, fish sauce, salt, pepper, sugar to taste and chicken stock. Bring to a boil. Cook another few minutes, remove from heat and serve.

Helpful hint: The frogs' legs make a great appetizer when they're served hot and crispy.

OC NHOI THIT ☺☺☺

18 snails in shell
1 cup minced pork meat
2 tablespoons finely chopped wooden ear mushrooms
2 tablespoons finely chopped cellophane noodles
1 tablespoon diced shallots
1 tablespoon finely chopped lemongrass
Salt
Pepper
1 egg yolk
3 stalks lemongrass, cut in short lengths
1 cup Fish Sauce Dip (see page 37)

Boil (or steam) snails for 5 minutes. Remove the meat, mince, then mix together with the pork. Combine with mushrooms, noodles, shallots, lemongrass, salt and pepper to taste, and egg to bind the mixture. Stuff into shells and insert a small piece of lemongrass into each shell. Steam stuffed snails for another 5 minutes. Serve with Fish Sauce Dip.

Helpful hint: Canned snails are generally a good product and available in many supermarkets.

THIT HEO KHO TIEU & THIT HEO KHO NUOC DUA

Braised Pork with Fish Sauce & Pork Stew with Coconut Juice

THIT HEO KHO TIEU

Here are two quite different and delicious recipes featuring pork and *nuoc mam*. The combination is one of the unique characteristics of Vietnamese cuisine. ☉☉☉

- 1 pound boneless pork leg, sliced
- 1 cup water
- Freshly ground pepper

Marinade:
- 5 tablespoons fish sauce
- 1 tablespoon Caramel Syrup (see page 38)
- 2 tablespoons crushed pepper flakes
- 1 red chili
- 1 tablespoon sugar
- Salt

Marinate pork in the **marinade** ingredients for 1 hour. After marinating, place pork and **marinade** in a deep sauté pan. Bring to a boil, then reduce heat until liquid evaporates and add cup of water. Simmer, uncovered, until meat is cooked.

Garnish with freshly ground pepper. Serve with fresh vegetables and steamed rice.

Helpful hint: Coconut juice can be added instead of water.

THIT HEO KHO NUOC DUA ☉☉☉

- 2 pounds boneless pork leg, cut into 3-ounce pieces
- 3 tablespoons vegetable oil
- 4 cups young coconut juice
- 5 eggs, hard-boiled and peeled

Marinade:
- 4 cloves garlic, finely chopped
- Salt to taste
- 1 tablespoon palm sugar
- 4 tablespoons fish sauce

Combine **marinade** ingredients and marinate pork for 1 hour.

In either a wok or a frying pan, sear pork in heated oil. Add coconut juice. Skim the top, reduce heat and simmer until tender (30–45 minutes). Add the eggs and simmer another 15 minutes.

Serve with preserved bean sprouts, pickled or preserved mustard greens and steamed rice.

Helpful hint: Hard-boiled eggs appear in many Vietnamese dishes (absorbing the color of the sauce), but can be considered optional.

NEM NUONG & BUN THIT NUONG

Minced Pork Balls on a Skewer & Grilled Pork with Rice Noodles

NEM NUONG ☺☺☺

1 pound lean pork neck
1 teaspoon salt
8 ounces pork fatback
2 tablespoons sugar
2 cloves garlic, diced
2 red chilies, finely chopped
Salt to taste
1 tablespoon pepper
2 tablespoons ground roasted peanuts
$1/4$ cup Fish Sauce Dip (see page 37)

Garnish:

1 cup bean sprouts
2 medium starfruit, peeled and sliced
2 medium unripe bananas, thinly sliced
1 medium cucumber, peeled and sliced
1 head butter lettuce
1 cup mint leaves
20 pieces rice paper

Opposite: Minced
Pork Balls on a
Skewer (left) and
Grilled Pork with
Rice Noodles
(right).

Pound the pork meat with 1 teaspoon of salt to tenderise and set aside. Braise the pork fatback for 10 minutes, then cut into very small strips. Marinate with sugar, garlic, chili, salt and pepper for 5 minutes.

Combine the pork meats and shape into small balls. Place them on a bamboo skewer (3 or 4 to a skewer) and cook evenly over the charcoal grill. Sprinkle with peanuts, Fish Sauce Dip and **garnish**.

BUN THIT NUONG ☺☺☺

1 pound pork loin, cut into medium cubes

Marinade:

1 teaspoon finely chopped garlic
$1/3$ cup sliced baby leeks or spring onions
3 tablespoons fish sauce
Pepper
Sugar

Garnish:

12 ounces rice noodles blanched
2 cups Carrot and Radish Pickles (see page 36)
1 cup bean sprouts
2 medium cucumbers, finely sliced
$1/2$ cup basil leaves
$1/3$ cup chopped baby leeks or spring onions
$1/4$ cup Peanut Sauce (see pages 37–38)

Combine the **marinade** ingredients and marinate pork for 20 minutes.

Skewer the pork and grill over charcoal. Turn frequently so that the pork is evenly cooked, and continue basting with the marinade. Serve with **garnish**.

Helpful hint: There are no set rules on how to eat the skewered meats. Once you remove the skewers, the large plate of garnish and various dipping sauces leave room for experimentation.

BO LA LOT

Grilled Beef in Wild Betel Leaves

The Vietnamese are famous for their hand rolls and almost every dinner features at least two or three different versions at the start of the meal. ①①①

1¼ pounds ground beef
10 ounces pork fatback
Salt
Sugar
21 wild betel leaves
7 wooden skewers
Vegetable oil

Marinade:

1 tablespoon five-spice powder
1 tablespoon curry powder
1 teaspoon turmeric powder
1 tablespoon sugar
1 tablespoon soy sauce
1 tablespoon finely chopped lemongrass
2 cloves garlic, finely chopped
1 teaspoon pepper

Garnish:

2 starfruit, thinly sliced
3 unripe bananas, thinly sliced
1 cucumber, peeled and thinly sliced
1 cup Fish Sauce Dip (see page 37)
Lettuce leaves for wrapping

Combine the **marinade** ingredients and marinate the beef for 30 minutes.

Fry pork fatback, allow to cool and then cut into fine slices (vermicelli size). Marinate with salt and sugar and set aside for 15 minutes. Soak wild betel leaves and drain.

Combine beef and pork fat, mix thoroughly, then wrap portions in wild betel leaf (the rolls should be roughly 2 inches long). Place 3 rolls on each skewer. Brush with oil and grill on both sides for 5 minutes, until the leaves are slightly charred. Serve with **garnish** and Fish Sauce Dip.

Helpful hints: You can also try adding fresh rice noodles into the wrap. Grape leaves may be substituted for the betel leaves.

BO KHO

Spicy Beef Stew

This is the Vietnamese variation on a traditional Western meal. ⏱ ⏱ ⏱

6 tablespoons cooking oil
2 tablespoons annatto seeds
2 pounds top round beef, cut into large cubes
1 large onion, finely chopped
5 cloves garlic, finely chopped
1 tablespoon salt
2 tablespoons sugar
1 tablespoon curry powder
1 cup beer
1 stalk lemongrass, bruised
3 pieces star anise
1 cinnamon stick
1 cup thickly chopped carrots

Garnish:

1 cup mint leaves
2 red chilies, sliced
Salt, Pepper and Lime mix (see page 39)

Heat half of the oil with annatto seeds and stir quickly until the oil takes on the reddish-brown color of the seeds. Set aside, strain and remove the seeds.

Marinate the beef cubes with onion, half the garlic, salt, sugar and half of the annatto seed oil mixture for 45 minutes.

Heat the remaining annatto seed oil and cook the remaining garlic until soft. Add curry powder, beer and marinade. Braise the beef, adding a little water, lemongrass, star anise and cinnamon. Before the meat is tender, add carrots. Simmer 3–5 minutes or until done. Serve with **garnish.**

Helpful hints: You may wish to remove the star anise before serving. This dish can easily be refrigerated and reheated the next day.

BO NHUNG DAM

Vietnamese Beef Hot Pot

This dish is traditionally served in a steam boat, set in the middle of the table. Good fun, informal dining—everyone helps themselves. ⏱ ⏱ ⏱

2 pounds beef tenderloin, sliced thinly
Salt
Pepper
Sugar

Dip:

1 cup vinegar
1 cup coconut juice
2 onions, finely sliced
3 tablespoons finely sliced lemongrass
2 tablespoons finely sliced and fried garlic
$^1/_2$ teaspoon salt
1 tablespoon sugar
$^1/_4$ teaspoon pepper

Garnish:

1 medium cucumber, peeled and sliced
$^1/_2$ cup pickled shallots
$^1/_2$ cup pickled vegetables
$^1/_2$ cup roasted peanuts, ground
$^1/_2$ cup chopped baby leeks or spring onions

1 cup Fermented Anchovy Dip (see page 37)
1 cup bean sprouts
1 medium head butter lettuce
2 starfruit, peeled and sliced
3 unripe bananas, sliced
3 cups fine rice noodles, blanched
20 pieces rice paper, softened

Marinate beef in salt, pepper and sugar, then set aside.

Combine **dip** ingredients in a large pan and bring to a boil. Reduce heat and simmer for 10 minutes. Begin dipping the beef.

Wrap cooked beef and some **garnish** in rice paper for dipping in anchovy dip and eating immediately.

Helpful hint: The best method for cooking the beef is to use long chopsticks. Since the slices are so thin, they should require only a few moments in the vinegar, unless you like your beef well done.

BANH GOI & BANH PHU THE

Wrapped Rice Cakes & Husband and Wife Cakes

BANH GOI ☻☻☻

1^3/$_4$ cups rice flour
1^1/$_3$ cups sugar
2^1/$_2$ cups pandan leaf juice
5 ounces yellow mung beans, soaked
2 tablespoons vanilla extract
1^1/$_2$ cups coconut milk
3 tablespoons sugar
1 pinch salt
1 tablespoon cornstarch
2 tablespoons cooking oil
6 banana leaves, blanched
2 tablespoons sesame seeds, toasted

Mix rice flour with ^{2}/$_3$ cup sugar and 2 cups pandan leaf juice. Cook over a low heat until mixture thickens to a paste-like consistency. In a separate pot, cook mung beans with remaining sugar and vanilla extract to a similar consistency. Cool down and roll into small balls.

Brush cooking oil on banana leaves, then place the rice flour paste in the middle. Top with mung bean "ball" and cover with rice flour paste. Wrap into small square packages and steam for 10 minutes.

To make the sauce, bring coconut milk to boil, add sugar, a pinch of salt, remaining pandan leaf juice and cornstarch.

Wrapped rice cakes are served with the coconut sauce and toasted sesame seeds.

BANH PHU THE

A traditional Vietnamese dessert from Hue. Its name comes from the two parts that are traditionally tied together with a string of coconut and encased in a delicate box (see page 126) made of pandan leaves. ☻☻☻

4 cups water
1 pound starch flour
1^1/$_3$ cups sugar
^{1}/$_2$ cup shredded coconut
5 ounces yellow mung beans, soaked in water
^{2}/$_3$ cup sugar syrup
1 tablespoon cooking oil
2 tablespoons pomelo blossom essence or lemon extract
20 pandan leaves (optional)

Dough: Mix water, flour, sugar and shredded coconut. Heat on a low flame and stir for 10 minutes.

Stuffing: Cook mung beans in water until they reach a pasty texture. Stir in sugar syrup and cooking oil. When much of the liquid begins to dry up, add pomelo blossom essence and remove from heat

Cooking: Put a thin layer of dough in individual cupcake tins or other small mold, add a portion of the stuffing and top with another layer of dough. Place tins in a steamer and cook for 20 minutes. When the dough is transparent, they are ready.

CHE CHUOI CHUNG & SUONG SA HOT LUU

Banana Sago Cream & Coconut and Four-Colored Drink

CHE CHUOI CHUNG ⏱⏱⏱

12 ripe bananas, peeled
1 cup sugar
$\frac{1}{2}$ cup sago, soaked and cooked
$\frac{1}{2}$ cup cassava dough, dried (*bit khoai*)
4 cups thin coconut milk
5 pandan leaves
1 cup thick coconut milk
Ground, roasted peanuts or toasted sesame
   seeds

Sprinkle bananas with sugar. Soak sago and cassava dough separately in water for 2 hours. In a saucepan, heat thin coconut milk with sago, cassava and pandan leaves for 15 minutes, then add the bananas. When bananas are done, add thick coconut milk and remove from heat. Allow to cool, arrange in bowls and sprinkle with peanuts (or toasted sesame seeds).

Opposite: Banana Sago Cream (left) and Coconut and Four-Colored Drink (right).

SUONG SA HOT LUU ⏱⏱⏱

1 ounce green mung bean paste
1 ounce agar agar
$1\frac{1}{2}$ ounce red and white tapioca
1 ounce green rice flour dumpling
$\frac{1}{3}$ cup thick coconut milk, chilled
$\frac{1}{4}$ cup sugar syrup, chilled
Ice cubes

Place all the above ingredients, one by one, in a glass. Then add the chilled sugar syrup and top with ice cubes.

Boxes (for Husband and Wife Cakes, on preceding page): Take an 8-inch leaf, divide it into 5 segments. Shape it into box and secure with a toothpick. Place a segment of pandan leaf in the box, then brush with cooking oil. Make the lids in the same fashion, but slightly bigger to cover the boxes. Then follow instructions on page 124.

BANH CHUOI NUONG & BANH NUONG NHAN THOM

Banana Cake & Pineapple Tartlets

BANH CHUOI NUONG 🕐🕐🕐

1$^{1}/_{4}$ pounds ripe bananas
1 cup sugar
1 cup coconut milk
$^{1}/_{2}$ teaspoon vanilla extract
2 tablespoons melted butter
7 slices of sandwich bread

Slice the banana diagonally and sprinkle with half the sugar. Cook the remaining sugar in coconut milk until dissolved, then add the vanilla. Remove crusts from the bread. Soak the bread in the sweetened coconut milk.

Butter a 12-inch non stick pan. Arrange a layer of banana on the bottom of the pan. Cover with a layer of bread, then another layer of bananas, another bread layer, and then finish with a layer of bananas. Drizzle the remaining butter over the top, then cover with foil and bake in a preheated oven at 350°F for 1 hour. Rest for 12 hours before cutting.

Helpful hint: Serve with a scoop of vanilla ice cream.

BANH NUONG NHAN THOM 🕐🕐🕐

Dough:
1 cup soft butter
$^{1}/_{4}$ cup sugar
$^{1}/_{2}$ cup milk
4 cups flour

In a mixing bowl, blend butter, sugar and milk with a whisk. Add flour and continue whisking until the texture is smooth. Place the dough on a lightly floured surface and roll it out to a thickness of 1/8 inch with a rolling pin. Press dough into a small mold to make shells. Cut remaining dough into small strips.

Filling:
1 pineapple, peeled, cored and chopped
$^{1}/_{2}$ cup sugar
1 drop vanilla extract
1 egg, beaten

Place pineapple and sugar in a saucepan over a low heat and stir continuously until pineapple mixture thickens. Add vanilla extract. Fill shells with mixture, then lay dough strips in a crisscross over the tops of the tartlets. Brush the top with egg. Bake in oven, at 300°F, until golden brown.

Opposite: Banana Cake (left) and Pineapple Tartlets (right).

Mail-Order Sources of Ingredients

The ingredients found in this book can all be bought from markets featuring the foods of Vietnam. Many of them can also be found in markets featuring Asian foods, as well as any well-stocked supermarket. Ingredients not available locally may be available from the mail-order markets listed below.

Adriana's Caravan
409 Vanderbilt Street
Brooklyn, NY 11218
Tel: 800-316-0820 or 718-436-8565

Gourmail, Inc.
816 Newton Road
Berwyn, PA 19312
Tel: 215-296-4620

House of Spices
76-17 Broadway
Jackson Heights
Queens, NY 11373
Tel: 718-507-4900

Nancy's Speciality Market
PO Box 530
Newmarket, NH 03857
Tel: 800-462-6291

Oriental Food Market and Cooking School
2801 Howard Street
Chicago, IL 60645
Tel: 312-274-2826

Oriental Market
502 Pampas Drive
Austin, TX 78752
Tel: 512-453-9058

Pacific Mercantile Company
1925 Lawrence Street
Denver, CO 80202
Tel: 303-295-0293

Thailand Food Corp.
4821 N. Broadway Street
Chicago, IL 60640
Tel: 312-728-1199

Uwajimaya
PO Box 3003
Seattle, WA 98114
Tel: 206-624-6248

Vietnam Imports
922 Broad Street
Falls Church, VA 22046
Tel: 703-534-9441

Index